50 Saudi Arabian Recipes for Home

By: Kelly Johnson

Table of Contents

- Kabsa
- Mandi
- Shawarma
- Falafel
- Hummus
- Mutabbaq
- Samboosa
- Harees
- Jareesh
- Saleeg
- Thareed
- Kleeja
- Markook
- Shorbat Adas (Lentil Soup)
- Madfoon
- Ruz Bukhari (Bukhari Rice)
- Mathrooba
- Fatet Jaj (Chicken Fatet)
- Murtabak
- Lahoh
- Thareed Laham (Meat Thareed)
- Mutabbaq
- Kanafeh
- Basbousa
- Maamoul
- Khubz (Flatbread)
- Balaleet
- Harees Laham
- Ful Medames
- Luqaimat
- Jallab
- Jareesh Laham
- Jareesh Dajaj
- Martabak
- Samboosa Laham

- Dawood Basha
- Shish Tawook
- Molokhia
- Mutabbaq Laham
- Qursan
- Kabsa Dajaj
- Harraq Usfur
- Mathloutha
- Biryani
- Kleeja Tamr
- Kleeja Halwa
- Roz bil Khalta
- Harees Dajaj
- Murabyan
- Jareesh Halib

Kabsa

Ingredients:

- 2 cups basmati rice
- 500g chicken pieces (can also use lamb or goat)
- 2 onions, finely chopped
- 4 cloves garlic, minced
- 2 tomatoes, diced
- 1 carrot, diced
- 1 potato, diced
- 1 bell pepper, diced
- 2 tablespoons tomato paste
- 2 tablespoons Kabsa spice mix (a blend of spices including cardamom, cloves, cinnamon, black lime, nutmeg, and black pepper)
- Salt, to taste
- Vegetable oil, for cooking
- Chopped fresh cilantro or parsley, for garnish
- Lemon wedges, for serving

Instructions:

1. Rinse the basmati rice under cold water until the water runs clear. Drain and set aside.
2. Heat some vegetable oil in a large pot or Dutch oven over medium heat. Add the chopped onions and minced garlic, and sauté until softened and fragrant.
3. Add the chicken pieces to the pot and brown them on all sides.
4. Stir in the diced tomatoes, carrot, potato, and bell pepper. Cook for a few minutes until the vegetables start to soften.
5. Add the tomato paste and Kabsa spice mix to the pot, and stir until everything is well combined.
6. Pour in enough water to cover the chicken and vegetables. Bring the mixture to a boil, then reduce the heat to low and let it simmer for about 20-25 minutes, or until the chicken is cooked through and the vegetables are tender.
7. While the chicken is cooking, rinse the rice once again under cold water, then drain.
8. Once the chicken is cooked, remove it from the pot and set it aside. Measure the liquid in the pot – you'll need about 4 cups of liquid for every 2 cups of rice. Add more water if necessary.

9. Return the pot to the stove and bring the liquid to a boil. Stir in the drained rice and salt to taste. Reduce the heat to low, cover the pot, and let the rice simmer for about 15-20 minutes, or until it's cooked through and fluffy.
10. While the rice is cooking, preheat your oven to 350°F (175°C).
11. Once the rice is done, spread it out evenly in a baking dish. Arrange the cooked chicken pieces on top of the rice.
12. Cover the baking dish with aluminum foil and bake in the preheated oven for about 10-15 minutes to allow the flavors to meld together.
13. Serve the Kabsa hot, garnished with chopped fresh cilantro or parsley and lemon wedges on the side.

Enjoy this aromatic and flavorful Saudi Arabian dish with your family and friends! Adjust the spices and ingredients according to your taste preferences.

Kabsa

Ingredients:

- 2 cups basmati rice
- 500g chicken pieces (can also use lamb or goat)
- 2 onions, finely chopped
- 4 cloves garlic, minced
- 2 tomatoes, diced
- 1 carrot, diced
- 1 potato, diced
- 1 bell pepper, diced
- 2 tablespoons tomato paste
- 2 tablespoons Kabsa spice mix (a blend of spices including cardamom, cloves, cinnamon, black lime, nutmeg, and black pepper)
- Salt, to taste
- Vegetable oil, for cooking
- Chopped fresh cilantro or parsley, for garnish
- Lemon wedges, for serving

Instructions:

1. Rinse the basmati rice under cold water until the water runs clear. Drain and set aside.
2. Heat some vegetable oil in a large pot or Dutch oven over medium heat. Add the chopped onions and minced garlic, and sauté until softened and fragrant.
3. Add the chicken pieces to the pot and brown them on all sides.
4. Stir in the diced tomatoes, carrot, potato, and bell pepper. Cook for a few minutes until the vegetables start to soften.
5. Add the tomato paste and Kabsa spice mix to the pot, and stir until everything is well combined.
6. Pour in enough water to cover the chicken and vegetables. Bring the mixture to a boil, then reduce the heat to low and let it simmer for about 20-25 minutes, or until the chicken is cooked through and the vegetables are tender.
7. While the chicken is cooking, rinse the rice once again under cold water, then drain.
8. Once the chicken is cooked, remove it from the pot and set it aside. Measure the liquid in the pot – you'll need about 4 cups of liquid for every 2 cups of rice. Add more water if necessary.

9. Return the pot to the stove and bring the liquid to a boil. Stir in the drained rice and salt to taste. Reduce the heat to low, cover the pot, and let the rice simmer for about 15-20 minutes, or until it's cooked through and fluffy.
10. While the rice is cooking, preheat your oven to 350°F (175°C).
11. Once the rice is done, spread it out evenly in a baking dish. Arrange the cooked chicken pieces on top of the rice.
12. Cover the baking dish with aluminum foil and bake in the preheated oven for about 10-15 minutes to allow the flavors to meld together.
13. Serve the Kabsa hot, garnished with chopped fresh cilantro or parsley and lemon wedges on the side.

Enjoy this aromatic and flavorful Saudi Arabian dish with your family and friends! Adjust the spices and ingredients according to your taste preferences.

Mandi

Ingredients:

- 2 cups basmati rice
- 1 whole chicken (or pieces of chicken, lamb, or goat)
- 2 onions, finely chopped
- 4 cloves garlic, minced
- 2 tomatoes, diced
- 1 carrot, diced
- 1 potato, diced
- 1 bell pepper, diced
- 2 tablespoons tomato paste
- 2 tablespoons Mandi spice mix (a blend of spices including cardamom, cloves, cinnamon, black lime, nutmeg, and black pepper)
- Salt, to taste
- Vegetable oil, for cooking
- Chopped fresh cilantro or parsley, for garnish
- Lemon wedges, for serving

Instructions:

1. Rinse the basmati rice under cold water until the water runs clear. Drain and set aside.
2. If using a whole chicken, rub it with salt and Mandi spice mix, then let it marinate for at least 30 minutes.
3. Heat some vegetable oil in a large pot or Dutch oven over medium heat. Add the chopped onions and minced garlic, and sauté until softened and fragrant.
4. Add the chicken (or other meat) to the pot and brown it on all sides.
5. Stir in the diced tomatoes, carrot, potato, and bell pepper. Cook for a few minutes until the vegetables start to soften.
6. Add the tomato paste and Mandi spice mix to the pot, and stir until everything is well combined.
7. Pour in enough water to cover the chicken and vegetables. Bring the mixture to a boil, then reduce the heat to low and let it simmer for about 1-2 hours, or until the chicken is cooked through and tender (if using pieces of chicken, lamb, or goat, adjust the cooking time accordingly).

8. Once the meat is cooked, remove it from the pot and set it aside. Measure the liquid in the pot – you'll need about 4 cups of liquid for every 2 cups of rice. Add more water if necessary.
9. Return the pot to the stove and bring the liquid to a boil. Stir in the drained rice and salt to taste. Reduce the heat to low, cover the pot, and let the rice simmer for about 15-20 minutes, or until it's cooked through and fluffy.
10. While the rice is cooking, preheat your oven to 350°F (175°C).
11. Once the rice is done, spread it out evenly in a baking dish. Arrange the cooked meat on top of the rice.
12. Cover the baking dish with aluminum foil and bake in the preheated oven for about 10-15 minutes to allow the flavors to meld together.
13. Serve the Mandi hot, garnished with chopped fresh cilantro or parsley and lemon wedges on the side.

Enjoy this delicious and aromatic Saudi Arabian dish with your family and friends! Adjust the spices and ingredients according to your taste preferences.

Shawarma

Ingredients:

- 1 pound boneless, skinless chicken thighs or breasts
- 2 cloves garlic, minced
- 2 tablespoons lemon juice
- 2 tablespoons olive oil
- 1 teaspoon ground cumin
- 1 teaspoon ground paprika
- 1 teaspoon ground turmeric
- 1/2 teaspoon ground cinnamon
- 1/2 teaspoon ground coriander
- 1/4 teaspoon cayenne pepper (optional, for heat)
- Salt and black pepper, to taste
- Pita bread or flatbreads, for serving
- Toppings: chopped tomatoes, sliced cucumbers, shredded lettuce, sliced onions, pickles, etc.
- Sauces: tahini sauce, garlic sauce, hummus, etc.

Instructions:

1. In a bowl, whisk together the minced garlic, lemon juice, olive oil, ground cumin, paprika, turmeric, cinnamon, coriander, cayenne pepper (if using), salt, and black pepper.
2. Add the chicken thighs or breasts to the marinade and toss until evenly coated. Cover the bowl and refrigerate for at least 1 hour, or preferably overnight, to allow the flavors to meld.
3. Preheat your grill or grill pan over medium-high heat. Remove the chicken from the marinade and discard any excess marinade.
4. Grill the chicken for about 5-7 minutes per side, or until it's cooked through and nicely charred on the outside. Remove from the grill and let it rest for a few minutes before slicing.
5. Once rested, thinly slice the grilled chicken.
6. To assemble the shawarma wraps, warm the pita bread or flatbreads briefly on the grill or in a pan. Place some sliced chicken on each bread, along with your choice of toppings and sauces.
7. Roll up the bread tightly to enclose the filling, then wrap it in parchment paper or foil to hold it together.

8. Once the meat is cooked, remove it from the pot and set it aside. Measure the liquid in the pot – you'll need about 4 cups of liquid for every 2 cups of rice. Add more water if necessary.
9. Return the pot to the stove and bring the liquid to a boil. Stir in the drained rice and salt to taste. Reduce the heat to low, cover the pot, and let the rice simmer for about 15-20 minutes, or until it's cooked through and fluffy.
10. While the rice is cooking, preheat your oven to 350°F (175°C).
11. Once the rice is done, spread it out evenly in a baking dish. Arrange the cooked meat on top of the rice.
12. Cover the baking dish with aluminum foil and bake in the preheated oven for about 10-15 minutes to allow the flavors to meld together.
13. Serve the Mandi hot, garnished with chopped fresh cilantro or parsley and lemon wedges on the side.

Enjoy this delicious and aromatic Saudi Arabian dish with your family and friends! Adjust the spices and ingredients according to your taste preferences.

Shawarma

Ingredients:

- 1 pound boneless, skinless chicken thighs or breasts
- 2 cloves garlic, minced
- 2 tablespoons lemon juice
- 2 tablespoons olive oil
- 1 teaspoon ground cumin
- 1 teaspoon ground paprika
- 1 teaspoon ground turmeric
- 1/2 teaspoon ground cinnamon
- 1/2 teaspoon ground coriander
- 1/4 teaspoon cayenne pepper (optional, for heat)
- Salt and black pepper, to taste
- Pita bread or flatbreads, for serving
- Toppings: chopped tomatoes, sliced cucumbers, shredded lettuce, sliced onions, pickles, etc.
- Sauces: tahini sauce, garlic sauce, hummus, etc.

Instructions:

1. In a bowl, whisk together the minced garlic, lemon juice, olive oil, ground cumin, paprika, turmeric, cinnamon, coriander, cayenne pepper (if using), salt, and black pepper.
2. Add the chicken thighs or breasts to the marinade and toss until evenly coated. Cover the bowl and refrigerate for at least 1 hour, or preferably overnight, to allow the flavors to meld.
3. Preheat your grill or grill pan over medium-high heat. Remove the chicken from the marinade and discard any excess marinade.
4. Grill the chicken for about 5-7 minutes per side, or until it's cooked through and nicely charred on the outside. Remove from the grill and let it rest for a few minutes before slicing.
5. Once rested, thinly slice the grilled chicken.
6. To assemble the shawarma wraps, warm the pita bread or flatbreads briefly on the grill or in a pan. Place some sliced chicken on each bread, along with your choice of toppings and sauces.
7. Roll up the bread tightly to enclose the filling, then wrap it in parchment paper or foil to hold it together.

8. Serve the chicken shawarma wraps immediately, and enjoy!

Feel free to customize your chicken shawarma with your favorite toppings and sauces, and adjust the seasonings according to your taste preferences.

Falafel

Ingredients:

- 1 cup dried chickpeas, soaked overnight (or use canned chickpeas, drained and rinsed)
- 1 small onion, chopped
- 3 cloves garlic, minced
- 1/4 cup fresh parsley, chopped
- 1/4 cup fresh cilantro, chopped
- 1 teaspoon ground cumin
- 1 teaspoon ground coriander
- 1/2 teaspoon baking powder
- Salt and black pepper, to taste
- Vegetable oil, for frying

Instructions:

1. If using dried chickpeas, drain and rinse them after soaking overnight. Place the chickpeas in a food processor along with the chopped onion, minced garlic, fresh parsley, fresh cilantro, ground cumin, ground coriander, baking powder, salt, and black pepper.
2. Pulse the mixture in the food processor until it forms a coarse paste. Be careful not to over-process; you want the mixture to have some texture.
3. Transfer the falafel mixture to a bowl, cover, and refrigerate for at least 1 hour to allow the flavors to meld and the mixture to firm up.
4. Once chilled, shape the falafel mixture into small balls or patties, about 1 to 1.5 inches in diameter.
5. Heat vegetable oil in a deep fryer or large skillet to 350°F (175°C). Carefully add the falafel balls or patties to the hot oil in batches, making sure not to overcrowd the pan.
6. Fry the falafel for about 3-4 minutes per side, or until they are golden brown and crispy.
7. Remove the falafel from the oil using a slotted spoon and drain them on paper towels to remove excess oil.
8. Serve the falafel hot, inside pita bread or wrapped in flatbread, along with your choice of toppings and sauces, such as chopped tomatoes, shredded lettuce, sliced cucumbers, tahini sauce, or yogurt sauce.

Enjoy these delicious homemade falafel as a tasty and satisfying vegetarian option for lunch or dinner! Feel free to adjust the seasonings and add additional herbs or spices according to your taste preferences.

Hummus

Ingredients:

- 1 can (15 ounces) chickpeas (garbanzo beans), drained and rinsed
- 1/4 cup tahini (sesame paste)
- 3 tablespoons lemon juice (about 1 lemon)
- 2 cloves garlic, minced
- 2 tablespoons extra virgin olive oil, plus more for drizzling
- 1/2 teaspoon ground cumin
- Salt, to taste
- 2-3 tablespoons water, as needed
- Optional garnishes: chopped fresh parsley, paprika, pine nuts

Instructions:

1. In a food processor, combine the drained and rinsed chickpeas, tahini, lemon juice, minced garlic, olive oil, ground cumin, and a pinch of salt.
2. Process the mixture until smooth and creamy, scraping down the sides of the bowl as needed. If the hummus is too thick, add water, 1 tablespoon at a time, until you reach your desired consistency.
3. Taste the hummus and adjust the seasoning as needed, adding more salt or lemon juice if desired.
4. Transfer the hummus to a serving bowl. Drizzle with extra virgin olive oil and garnish with chopped fresh parsley, a sprinkle of paprika, and/or toasted pine nuts, if desired.
5. Serve the hummus with pita bread, crackers, sliced vegetables, or as a spread on sandwiches or wraps.

Enjoy this homemade hummus as a delicious and nutritious dip or spread! Experiment with additional ingredients such as roasted red peppers, sun-dried tomatoes, or fresh herbs to create your own unique variations.

Mutabbaq

Ingredients:

For the Dough:

- 2 cups all-purpose flour
- 1/2 teaspoon salt
- 1/2 cup warm water
- 2 tablespoons vegetable oil

For the Filling:

- 1/2 pound ground beef or lamb
- 1 onion, finely chopped
- 2 cloves garlic, minced
- 1 teaspoon ground cumin
- 1 teaspoon ground coriander
- 1/2 teaspoon ground turmeric
- 1/2 teaspoon chili powder (optional, for heat)
- Salt and black pepper, to taste
- Vegetable oil, for frying

Instructions:

1. In a large mixing bowl, combine the all-purpose flour and salt. Gradually add the warm water and vegetable oil, and knead the dough until it's smooth and elastic. Cover the dough with a clean kitchen towel and let it rest for about 30 minutes.
2. While the dough is resting, prepare the filling. In a skillet or frying pan, heat some vegetable oil over medium heat. Add the chopped onion and minced garlic, and sauté until softened and fragrant.
3. Add the ground beef or lamb to the skillet and cook until browned, breaking it up with a spoon as it cooks.
4. Stir in the ground cumin, ground coriander, ground turmeric, chili powder (if using), salt, and black pepper. Cook for a few more minutes until the spices are fragrant and the filling is well combined. Remove from heat and let it cool slightly.
5. Divide the rested dough into equal-sized balls. Roll out each ball into a thin circle on a lightly floured surface.

6. Place a spoonful of the filling onto one half of each dough circle, leaving a border around the edges.
7. Fold the other half of the dough over the filling to create a half-moon shape. Press the edges firmly to seal.
8. Heat some vegetable oil in a skillet or frying pan over medium heat. Carefully place the filled dough into the hot oil and fry on both sides until golden brown and crispy.
9. Remove the Mutabbaq from the oil and drain on paper towels to remove excess oil.
10. Serve the Mutabbaq hot, cut into wedges, and enjoy!

You can serve Mutabbaq as a delicious appetizer, snack, or even as a main dish. Feel free to customize the filling with your favorite ingredients and spices to suit your taste preferences.

Samboosa

Ingredients:

For the Dough:

- 2 cups all-purpose flour
- 1/2 teaspoon salt
- 1/4 cup vegetable oil
- 1/2 cup warm water

For the Filling:

- 1 medium potato, peeled and diced
- 1/2 cup frozen peas
- 1 carrot, peeled and diced
- 1 small onion, finely chopped
- 2 cloves garlic, minced
- 1 teaspoon ground cumin
- 1 teaspoon ground coriander
- 1/2 teaspoon ground turmeric
- 1/2 teaspoon chili powder (optional, for heat)
- Salt and black pepper, to taste
- Vegetable oil, for frying

Instructions:

1. In a large mixing bowl, combine the all-purpose flour and salt. Gradually add the vegetable oil and warm water, and knead the dough until it's smooth and elastic. Cover the dough with a clean kitchen towel and let it rest for about 30 minutes.
2. While the dough is resting, prepare the filling. In a pot of boiling water, cook the diced potato, peas, and carrot until they are tender. Drain and set aside.
3. In a skillet or frying pan, heat some vegetable oil over medium heat. Add the chopped onion and minced garlic, and sauté until softened and fragrant.
4. Add the cooked vegetables to the skillet along with the ground cumin, ground coriander, ground turmeric, chili powder (if using), salt, and black pepper. Cook for a few more minutes until the spices are fragrant and the filling is well combined. Remove from heat and let it cool slightly.

5. Divide the rested dough into equal-sized balls. Roll out each ball into a thin circle on a lightly floured surface.
6. Cut each circle of dough in half to create two semi-circles.
7. Place a spoonful of the filling onto one half of each semi-circle, leaving a border around the edges.
8. Fold the other half of the dough over the filling to create a triangle shape. Press the edges firmly to seal.
9. Heat some vegetable oil in a skillet or frying pan over medium heat. Carefully place the filled dough triangles into the hot oil and fry on both sides until golden brown and crispy.
10. Remove the Samboosa from the oil and drain on paper towels to remove excess oil.
11. Serve the Samboosa hot, and enjoy!

You can serve Samboosa as a delicious appetizer, snack, or even as part of a meal. Feel free to customize the filling with your favorite ingredients and spices to suit your taste preferences. Additionally, you can bake the Samboosa instead of frying for a healthier option.

Harees

Ingredients:

- 1 cup whole wheat berries
- 1/2 pound boneless chicken or lamb, cut into small pieces
- 1 onion, finely chopped
- 2 cloves garlic, minced
- 4 cups water or chicken broth
- Salt, to taste
- Ground black pepper, to taste
- Ground cinnamon, to taste
- Ground cardamom, to taste
- Ghee or butter, for serving
- Optional garnishes: fried onions, chopped fresh cilantro or parsley, ground cumin

Instructions:

1. Rinse the whole wheat berries under cold water until the water runs clear. Drain and set aside.
2. In a large pot, combine the rinsed wheat berries, chicken or lamb pieces, chopped onion, minced garlic, water or chicken broth, salt, black pepper, cinnamon, and cardamom.
3. Bring the mixture to a boil over medium-high heat, then reduce the heat to low and simmer, covered, for about 1 to 1.5 hours, or until the wheat berries and meat are very soft and tender. Stir occasionally to prevent sticking.
4. Once the wheat berries and meat are cooked through, use a hand blender or potato masher to mash them into a smooth and creamy consistency. Alternatively, you can transfer the mixture to a blender and blend until smooth.
5. Taste the Harees and adjust the seasoning as needed, adding more salt, pepper, cinnamon, or cardamom to taste.
6. Serve the Harees hot, drizzled with ghee or butter and garnished with fried onions, chopped fresh cilantro or parsley, and a sprinkle of ground cumin, if desired.

Enjoy this comforting and nourishing Harees as a hearty meal on its own, or serve it alongside flatbread, yogurt, or salad for a complete and satisfying dish. Feel free to adjust the seasonings and garnishes according to your taste preferences.

Jareesh

Ingredients:

- 1 cup cracked wheat (Jareesh)
- 1/2 pound boneless chicken or lamb, cut into small pieces
- 1 onion, finely chopped
- 2 cloves garlic, minced
- 4 cups water or chicken broth
- Salt, to taste
- Ground black pepper, to taste
- Ground cinnamon, to taste
- Ground cardamom, to taste
- Ghee or butter, for serving
- Optional garnishes: fried onions, chopped fresh cilantro or parsley, ground cumin

Instructions:

1. Rinse the cracked wheat (Jareesh) under cold water until the water runs clear. Drain and set aside.
2. In a large pot, combine the rinsed cracked wheat, chicken or lamb pieces, chopped onion, minced garlic, water or chicken broth, salt, black pepper, cinnamon, and cardamom.
3. Bring the mixture to a boil over medium-high heat, then reduce the heat to low and simmer, covered, for about 1 to 1.5 hours, or until the cracked wheat and meat are very soft and tender. Stir occasionally to prevent sticking.
4. Once the cracked wheat and meat are cooked through, use a hand blender or potato masher to mash them into a smooth and creamy consistency. Alternatively, you can transfer the mixture to a blender and blend until smooth.
5. Taste the Jareesh and adjust the seasoning as needed, adding more salt, pepper, cinnamon, or cardamom to taste.
6. Serve the Jareesh hot, drizzled with ghee or butter and garnished with fried onions, chopped fresh cilantro or parsley, and a sprinkle of ground cumin, if desired.

Enjoy this comforting and nourishing Jareesh as a hearty meal on its own, or serve it alongside flatbread, yogurt, or salad for a complete and satisfying dish. Feel free to adjust the seasonings and garnishes according to your taste preferences.

Saleeg

Ingredients:

- 2 cups white rice
- 6 cups chicken broth
- 2 cups water
- 1 teaspoon salt, or to taste
- 1/2 teaspoon ground white pepper
- 1/2 cup milk or heavy cream
- Ghee or butter, for serving
- Optional toppings: shredded chicken, fried onions, ground cinnamon, chopped fresh cilantro or parsley

Instructions:

1. In a large pot, combine the white rice, chicken broth, water, salt, and ground white pepper. Bring the mixture to a boil over medium-high heat.
2. Once boiling, reduce the heat to low and simmer, covered, for about 30-40 minutes, or until the rice is cooked through and soft, and the mixture has thickened to a creamy consistency. Stir occasionally to prevent sticking.
3. Once the rice is cooked, stir in the milk or heavy cream to add richness and creaminess to the dish. Adjust the seasoning with salt and pepper, if needed.
4. Serve the Saleeg hot, drizzled with ghee or butter, and topped with optional toppings such as shredded chicken, fried onions, ground cinnamon, and chopped fresh cilantro or parsley.

Enjoy this comforting and nourishing Saleeg as a satisfying meal on its own, or serve it alongside grilled or roasted meats, vegetables, or salads. Feel free to customize the toppings and seasonings according to your taste preferences.

Thareed

Ingredients:

- 1 pound lamb or chicken, cut into bite-sized pieces
- 2 tablespoons vegetable oil
- 1 onion, finely chopped
- 2 cloves garlic, minced
- 2 tomatoes, chopped
- 1 teaspoon ground cumin
- 1 teaspoon ground coriander
- 1/2 teaspoon ground turmeric
- Salt and black pepper, to taste
- 4 cups chicken or beef broth
- 4 pieces of flatbread (such as pita or khubz), torn into bite-sized pieces
- 2 cups chopped vegetables (such as carrots, potatoes, zucchini, or bell peppers)
- Chopped fresh cilantro or parsley, for garnish

Instructions:

1. In a large pot or Dutch oven, heat the vegetable oil over medium heat. Add the chopped onion and minced garlic, and sauté until softened and fragrant.
2. Add the lamb or chicken pieces to the pot and cook until browned on all sides.
3. Stir in the chopped tomatoes, ground cumin, ground coriander, ground turmeric, salt, and black pepper. Cook for a few minutes until the tomatoes start to break down and the spices are fragrant.
4. Pour in the chicken or beef broth and bring the mixture to a simmer. Let it simmer for about 30 minutes to allow the flavors to meld and the meat to become tender.
5. Once the meat is tender, add the torn flatbread pieces to the pot, stirring gently to combine and submerge the bread in the broth.
6. Add the chopped vegetables to the pot, making sure they are submerged in the broth. Simmer for an additional 15-20 minutes, or until the vegetables are cooked through.
7. Taste the Thareed and adjust the seasoning with salt and pepper, if needed.
8. Serve the Thareed hot, garnished with chopped fresh cilantro or parsley.

Enjoy this comforting and hearty Thareed as a delicious and satisfying meal. Feel free to customize the ingredients and seasonings according to your taste preferences.

Kleeja

Ingredients:

- 2 cups all-purpose flour
- 1 cup unsalted butter, softened
- 1 cup granulated sugar
- 1 egg
- 1 teaspoon ground cardamom
- 1/2 teaspoon ground cinnamon
- 1/4 teaspoon ground cloves
- 1/4 teaspoon ground nutmeg
- Pinch of salt
- 1/4 cup chopped nuts (such as almonds or pistachios), optional
- Powdered sugar, for dusting (optional)

Instructions:

1. Preheat your oven to 350°F (175°C). Line a baking sheet with parchment paper or lightly grease it.
2. In a mixing bowl, cream together the softened butter and granulated sugar until light and fluffy.
3. Add the egg to the butter-sugar mixture and beat until well combined.
4. In a separate bowl, sift together the all-purpose flour, ground cardamom, ground cinnamon, ground cloves, ground nutmeg, and pinch of salt.
5. Gradually add the dry ingredients to the wet ingredients, mixing until a smooth dough forms. If using chopped nuts, fold them into the dough at this point.
6. Divide the dough into small portions and shape each portion into a ball. Place the dough balls onto the prepared baking sheet, leaving some space between them as they will spread slightly during baking.
7. Flatten each dough ball slightly with the palm of your hand or the bottom of a glass to form a disc shape.
8. Using a knife or a cookie cutter, make decorative cuts or patterns on the surface of each cookie.
9. Bake the Kleeja cookies in the preheated oven for about 12-15 minutes, or until they are lightly golden brown around the edges.
10. Remove the cookies from the oven and let them cool on the baking sheet for a few minutes before transferring them to a wire rack to cool completely.

11. Once cooled, dust the Kleeja cookies with powdered sugar, if desired, before serving.

Enjoy these aromatic and delicious Kleeja cookies with a cup of tea or coffee for a delightful sweet treat! Store any leftovers in an airtight container at room temperature for up to a week.

Markook

Ingredients:

- 3 cups all-purpose flour, plus more for dusting
- 1 teaspoon salt
- 1 tablespoon olive oil
- 1 cup warm water

Instructions:

1. In a large mixing bowl, combine the all-purpose flour and salt.
2. Gradually add the warm water and olive oil to the flour mixture, stirring until a dough begins to form.
3. Turn the dough out onto a lightly floured surface and knead it for about 5-7 minutes, or until it becomes smooth and elastic. Add more flour if necessary to prevent sticking.
4. Divide the dough into 6-8 equal-sized portions and shape each portion into a ball. Cover the dough balls with a clean kitchen towel and let them rest for about 15-20 minutes.
5. After the resting period, one at a time, roll out each dough ball into a very thin circle, about 12-14 inches (30-35 cm) in diameter. Dust the work surface and rolling pin with flour as needed to prevent sticking.
6. Heat a large non-stick skillet or griddle over medium-high heat. Once hot, carefully transfer one of the rolled-out dough circles to the skillet and cook for about 1-2 minutes on each side, or until lightly browned and bubbles begin to form.
7. Remove the cooked Markook bread from the skillet and place it on a clean kitchen towel. Cover the bread with the towel to keep it warm and soft while you cook the remaining dough circles.
8. Repeat the process with the remaining dough balls, rolling them out and cooking them one by one.
9. Serve the Markook bread warm, either folded or rolled up, as a side dish or as a wrap for sandwiches, kebabs, or other fillings.

Enjoy this homemade Markook bread as a versatile and delicious addition to your

Middle Eastern-inspired meals! Adjust the thickness of the bread according to your preference, and experiment with different fillings and toppings to create your own unique variations.

Shorbat Adas (Lentil Soup)

Ingredients:

- 1 cup dried red lentils, rinsed and drained
- 1 onion, finely chopped
- 2 carrots, peeled and diced
- 2 celery stalks, diced
- 2 cloves garlic, minced
- 1 teaspoon ground cumin
- 1 teaspoon ground coriander
- 1/2 teaspoon ground turmeric
- 6 cups vegetable or chicken broth
- Salt and black pepper, to taste
- Juice of 1 lemon
- Chopped fresh parsley or cilantro, for garnish
- Extra virgin olive oil, for drizzling (optional)

Instructions:

1. In a large pot, heat a drizzle of olive oil over medium heat. Add the chopped onion, carrots, and celery, and sauté until softened, about 5-7 minutes.
2. Add the minced garlic, ground cumin, ground coriander, and ground turmeric to the pot, and cook for another 1-2 minutes, or until the spices are fragrant.
3. Add the rinsed red lentils to the pot, followed by the vegetable or chicken broth. Bring the mixture to a boil, then reduce the heat to low and let it simmer, covered, for about 20-25 minutes, or until the lentils are tender and cooked through.
4. Once the lentils are cooked, use an immersion blender to blend the soup until smooth and creamy. Alternatively, you can transfer the soup to a blender in batches and blend until smooth, then return it to the pot.
5. Season the soup with salt and black pepper, to taste. If the soup is too thick, you can add more broth or water to reach your desired consistency.
6. Stir in the lemon juice, adjusting the amount to your taste preference.
7. Serve the Shorbat Adas hot, garnished with chopped fresh parsley or cilantro, and a drizzle of extra virgin olive oil, if desired.
8. Enjoy this comforting and nutritious Lentil Soup as a starter or as a main dish, served with crusty bread or alongside a salad.

Feel free to customize this Shorbat Adas recipe by adding other vegetables or spices according to your taste preferences. You can also top the soup with a dollop of yogurt or a sprinkle of chili flakes for extra flavor.

Madfoon

Ingredients:

- 2 pounds lamb or chicken, cut into large pieces
- 2 cups basmati rice, rinsed and drained
- 4 cups water
- 2 onions, finely chopped
- 4 cloves garlic, minced
- 2 tomatoes, chopped
- 2 carrots, peeled and diced
- 2 potatoes, peeled and diced
- 1/2 cup chopped fresh cilantro or parsley
- 1/4 cup vegetable oil
- 1 tablespoon Arabic spice mix (Baharat)
- 1 teaspoon ground cumin
- 1 teaspoon ground coriander
- 1 teaspoon ground turmeric
- Salt and black pepper, to taste
- Saffron threads, soaked in warm water (optional, for coloring and flavor)
- Whole spices (such as cinnamon sticks, cardamom pods, and cloves), for flavoring

Instructions:

1. In a large pot or Dutch oven, heat the vegetable oil over medium heat. Add the chopped onions and minced garlic, and sauté until softened and golden brown.
2. Add the chopped tomatoes to the pot and cook until they start to break down and release their juices.
3. Add the Arabic spice mix (Baharat), ground cumin, ground coriander, and ground turmeric to the pot, stirring to coat the onions and tomatoes with the spices.
4. Add the meat pieces to the pot and brown them on all sides, stirring occasionally.
5. Once the meat is browned, add enough water to cover the meat in the pot. Bring the mixture to a boil, then reduce the heat to low and let it simmer, covered, for about 1 to 1.5 hours, or until the meat is tender and cooked through.
6. While the meat is cooking, prepare the rice. In a separate pot, bring the 4 cups of water to a boil. Add the rinsed and drained basmati rice to the boiling water, along with the diced carrots and potatoes. Season with salt and black pepper, to taste.

7. Reduce the heat to low, cover the pot, and let the rice simmer for about 15-20 minutes, or until the rice is cooked through and fluffy.
8. Once the meat is tender, remove it from the pot and set it aside. Strain the cooking liquid to remove any solids and set the liquid aside.
9. In the same pot used to cook the meat, layer the cooked rice and vegetables on the bottom. Place the cooked meat pieces on top of the rice.
10. Pour the reserved cooking liquid over the meat and rice layers, ensuring that everything is evenly moistened. Add the soaked saffron threads, if using, for color and flavor.
11. Cover the pot tightly with a lid or aluminum foil, and let the Madfoon cook over low heat for another 20-30 minutes, or until the flavors have melded together and the rice is infused with the meaty goodness.
12. Once done, garnish the Madfoon with chopped fresh cilantro or parsley before serving.

Serve the Madfoon hot, family-style, on a large platter, allowing everyone to dig in and enjoy the delicious flavors of this traditional Saudi Arabian dish. Pair it with some Arabic salad, yogurt, or pickles for a complete and satisfying meal.

Ruz Bukhari (Bukhari Rice)

Ingredients:

- 2 cups basmati rice, rinsed and drained
- 1 pound lamb or chicken, cut into large pieces
- 2 onions, thinly sliced
- 4 cloves garlic, minced
- 2 tomatoes, chopped
- 2 carrots, peeled and diced
- 2 potatoes, peeled and diced
- 1/2 cup raisins (optional)
- 1/4 cup vegetable oil or ghee
- 4 cups water or chicken broth
- 1 teaspoon Arabic spice mix (Baharat)
- 1 teaspoon ground cumin
- 1 teaspoon ground coriander
- 1 teaspoon ground turmeric
- Salt and black pepper, to taste
- Whole spices (such as cinnamon sticks, cardamom pods, and cloves), for flavoring
- Chopped fresh cilantro or parsley, for garnish

Instructions:

1. In a large pot or Dutch oven, heat the vegetable oil or ghee over medium heat. Add the thinly sliced onions and cook, stirring occasionally, until they are caramelized and golden brown. This may take about 20-30 minutes. Remove about half of the caramelized onions from the pot and set them aside for later use as a garnish.
2. To the remaining caramelized onions in the pot, add the minced garlic, chopped tomatoes, and Arabic spice mix (Baharat), ground cumin, ground coriander, and ground turmeric. Cook for a few minutes until the tomatoes start to break down and release their juices.
3. Add the lamb or chicken pieces to the pot and brown them on all sides, stirring occasionally.
4. Once the meat is browned, add the diced carrots, potatoes, and raisins (if using) to the pot. Stir to combine.

5. Add the rinsed and drained basmati rice to the pot, followed by the water or chicken broth. Season with salt and black pepper, to taste. Stir gently to combine all the ingredients.
6. Bring the mixture to a boil, then reduce the heat to low and let it simmer, covered, for about 15-20 minutes, or until the rice is cooked through and fluffy and the meat is tender.
7. Once the Ruz Bukhari is done cooking, fluff the rice with a fork and transfer it to a serving platter.
8. Garnish the Ruz Bukhari with the reserved caramelized onions and chopped fresh cilantro or parsley.
9. Serve the Ruz Bukhari hot, accompanied by some Arabic salad, yogurt, or pickles for a complete and satisfying meal.

Enjoy the rich and aromatic flavors of this traditional Saudi Arabian Bukhari Rice dish, perfect for sharing with family and friends on special occasions or as a comforting meal any day of the week. Adjust the spices and seasonings according to your taste preferences.

Mathrooba

Ingredients:

- 1 cup whole wheat berries (cracked wheat can be used as a substitute)
- 1 pound lamb or chicken, cut into small pieces
- 1 onion, finely chopped
- 3 cloves garlic, minced
- 2 tomatoes, chopped
- 2 tablespoons tomato paste
- 1 tablespoon Arabic spice mix (Baharat)
- 1 teaspoon ground turmeric
- 1 teaspoon ground cumin
- 1/2 teaspoon ground coriander
- 6 cups water or chicken broth
- Salt and black pepper, to taste
- Chopped fresh cilantro or parsley, for garnish

Instructions:

1. In a large pot, combine the whole wheat berries with water or chicken broth. Bring to a boil over medium-high heat, then reduce the heat to low and let it simmer, covered, for about 30 minutes, or until the wheat berries are soft and cooked through. If using cracked wheat, adjust the cooking time accordingly.
2. While the wheat is cooking, heat a little oil in a separate pan over medium heat. Add the chopped onion and minced garlic, and sauté until softened and fragrant.
3. Add the chopped tomatoes, tomato paste, Arabic spice mix, ground turmeric, ground cumin, and ground coriander to the pan. Cook for a few minutes until the tomatoes break down and the spices are fragrant.
4. Add the chopped lamb or chicken pieces to the pan and cook until browned on all sides.
5. Once the wheat berries are cooked, use a potato masher or immersion blender to mash them into a smooth paste.
6. Add the mashed wheat mixture to the pan with the cooked meat and spices. Stir to combine.
7. Gradually add the water or chicken broth to the mixture, stirring constantly to prevent lumps from forming.
8. Bring the mixture to a simmer and let it cook, uncovered, for about 15-20 minutes, or until it thickens to your desired consistency.

9. Season the Mathrooba with salt and black pepper, to taste.
10. Serve the Mathrooba hot, garnished with chopped fresh cilantro or parsley.

Enjoy the rich and comforting flavors of Mathrooba as a hearty meal, served with bread or rice. Adjust the spices and seasonings according to your taste preferences.

Fatet Jaj (Chicken Fatet)

Ingredients:

- 1 whole chicken, cut into pieces
- 2 cups plain yogurt
- 4 cloves garlic, minced
- 2 cups chicken broth
- 4 cups day-old bread, torn into bite-sized pieces
- 1 cup long-grain rice or vermicelli noodles, cooked
- 1/2 cup pine nuts or slivered almonds, toasted
- 2 tablespoons butter or olive oil
- 1 teaspoon ground cinnamon
- 1 teaspoon ground allspice
- Salt and black pepper, to taste
- Chopped fresh parsley or cilantro, for garnish

Instructions:

1. In a large pot, bring the chicken pieces to a boil in enough water to cover them. Reduce the heat and simmer until the chicken is cooked through, about 30-40 minutes. Remove the chicken from the pot and let it cool slightly. Shred or chop the chicken into bite-sized pieces, discarding the skin and bones.
2. In a separate bowl, whisk together the plain yogurt, minced garlic, and a pinch of salt. Set aside.
3. In a large skillet, melt the butter or heat the olive oil over medium heat. Add the torn bread pieces and toast them until golden brown and crispy. Remove from the skillet and set aside.
4. In the same skillet, add the cooked rice or vermicelli noodles and toast until lightly golden and fragrant. Remove from the skillet and set aside.
5. In the same skillet, add the shredded chicken pieces along with the ground cinnamon and ground allspice. Season with salt and black pepper to taste. Cook until the chicken is heated through and well coated with the spices.
6. To assemble the Fatet Jaj, spread half of the toasted bread pieces on the bottom of a serving dish. Top with half of the toasted rice or vermicelli noodles, followed by half of the spiced chicken.
7. Pour half of the yogurt mixture over the chicken layer, spreading it evenly. Repeat the layers with the remaining toasted bread, rice or vermicelli noodles, chicken, and yogurt mixture.

8. Sprinkle the toasted pine nuts or slivered almonds over the top of the Fatet Jaj.
9. Garnish with chopped fresh parsley or cilantro before serving.

Fatet Jaj is best served warm, allowing all the flavors to meld together. Enjoy this comforting and flavorful dish as a main course for lunch or dinner, and savor the delicious combination of textures and spices. Adjust the seasoning and garnishes according to your taste preferences.

Murtabak

Ingredients:

- 2 cups all-purpose flour
- 1/2 teaspoon salt
- 1/2 cup water
- 1 egg
- Vegetable oil, for frying

Filling:

- 1 pound ground beef or chicken
- 1 onion, finely chopped
- 2 cloves garlic, minced
- 1 teaspoon ground coriander
- 1 teaspoon ground cumin
- 1/2 teaspoon ground turmeric
- 1/2 teaspoon chili powder (optional)
- Salt and black pepper, to taste
- 2 eggs, beaten
- Chopped fresh cilantro or parsley, for garnish

Instructions:

1. In a mixing bowl, combine the all-purpose flour and salt. Gradually add the water and egg, stirring until a smooth dough forms. Knead the dough for a few minutes until it's soft and elastic. Cover with a clean kitchen towel and let it rest for about 30 minutes.
2. While the dough is resting, prepare the filling. In a skillet, heat a little vegetable oil over medium heat. Add the chopped onion and minced garlic, and sauté until softened and fragrant.
3. Add the ground beef or chicken to the skillet and cook until browned, breaking it up with a spoon as it cooks.
4. Stir in the ground coriander, ground cumin, ground turmeric, chili powder (if using), salt, and black pepper. Cook for another few minutes until the spices are fragrant and well combined with the meat mixture. Remove from heat and let it cool slightly.

5. Divide the dough into equal-sized balls. Roll out each ball into a thin circle on a lightly floured surface.
6. Spoon a portion of the meat filling onto one half of each dough circle, leaving a small border around the edges.
7. Fold the other half of the dough over the filling to enclose it, pressing the edges together to seal.
8. Heat a little vegetable oil in a skillet over medium heat. Carefully transfer the stuffed dough to the skillet and cook until golden brown and crispy on both sides, flipping halfway through. Repeat with the remaining dough and filling.
9. Once cooked, transfer the Murtabak to a serving platter and garnish with chopped fresh cilantro or parsley.
10. Serve the Murtabak hot, accompanied by a tangy dipping sauce or a side of pickled vegetables.

Enjoy this delicious and satisfying Murtabak as a snack or a main dish, and savor the flavorful filling wrapped in crispy, golden-brown dough. Feel free to customize the filling with your favorite ingredients and spices.

Lahoh

Ingredients:

- 2 cups all-purpose flour
- 1 cup semolina flour (optional, for added texture)
- 1 teaspoon active dry yeast
- 1 teaspoon sugar
- 1 teaspoon salt
- 2 cups warm water
- Vegetable oil, for cooking

Instructions:

1. In a large mixing bowl, combine the all-purpose flour, semolina flour (if using), active dry yeast, sugar, and salt.
2. Gradually add the warm water to the dry ingredients, stirring continuously to form a smooth batter. The consistency should be similar to that of pancake batter. Cover the bowl with a clean kitchen towel and let it rest at room temperature for about 1-2 hours, or until the batter has doubled in volume and is bubbly.
3. After the resting period, gently stir the batter to deflate it slightly.
4. Heat a non-stick skillet or griddle over medium heat. Lightly grease the surface with vegetable oil.
5. Pour a ladleful of the batter onto the skillet, spreading it out into a thin, round shape using the back of the ladle. Cook for 2-3 minutes, or until the edges start to lift and the surface is covered with small bubbles.
6. Carefully flip the Lahoh using a spatula and cook for another 1-2 minutes on the other side, until lightly golden brown.
7. Remove the cooked Lahoh from the skillet and transfer it to a plate. Repeat the process with the remaining batter, adding more oil to the skillet as needed.
8. Serve the Lahoh warm, accompanied by honey, ghee, or your favorite sauce.

Enjoy the soft and spongy texture of Lahoh as a delightful breakfast or snack.

Experiment with different toppings and fillings to create your own unique variations.

Thareed Laham (Meat Thareed)

Ingredients:

- 1 pound lamb or beef stew meat, cut into chunks
- 2 onions, chopped
- 4 cloves garlic, minced
- 2 tomatoes, chopped
- 2 carrots, peeled and diced
- 2 potatoes, peeled and diced
- 1 zucchini, diced
- 1 cup chickpeas, cooked (canned chickpeas can be used)
- 6 cups water or beef broth
- 2 tablespoons tomato paste
- 2 tablespoons olive oil
- 1 teaspoon ground cumin
- 1 teaspoon ground coriander
- 1 teaspoon ground turmeric
- 1/2 teaspoon ground cinnamon
- Salt and black pepper, to taste
- Fresh cilantro or parsley, chopped, for garnish
- Flatbread or pita bread, toasted or torn into pieces

Instructions:

1. In a large pot or Dutch oven, heat the olive oil over medium heat. Add the chopped onions and minced garlic, and sauté until softened and fragrant.
2. Add the chunks of lamb or beef to the pot and cook until browned on all sides.
3. Stir in the chopped tomatoes, tomato paste, ground cumin, ground coriander, ground turmeric, ground cinnamon, salt, and black pepper. Cook for a few minutes until the tomatoes start to break down and release their juices.
4. Add the diced carrots, potatoes, zucchini, and cooked chickpeas to the pot. Pour in the water or beef broth, making sure all the ingredients are submerged.
5. Bring the mixture to a boil, then reduce the heat to low and let it simmer, covered, for about 1 to 1.5 hours, or until the meat is tender and the vegetables are cooked through.
6. Once the stew is cooked, use a slotted spoon to remove the meat and vegetables from the pot and set them aside. Skim off any excess fat from the surface of the broth.

7. To serve, arrange pieces of toasted or torn flatbread or pita bread in a serving dish. Ladle the meat and vegetable mixture over the bread, making sure to moisten the bread with some of the broth.
8. Garnish the Thareed Laham with chopped fresh cilantro or parsley before serving.

Enjoy the comforting and aromatic flavors of Meat Thareed with its tender chunks of meat, hearty vegetables, and fragrant spices. Serve it as a main course for lunch or dinner, accompanied by a side of yogurt or a simple salad. Adjust the seasoning and spices according to your taste preferences.

Mutabbaq

Ingredients:

- 2 cups all-purpose flour
- 1/2 teaspoon salt
- 3/4 cup warm water
- Vegetable oil, for frying

Filling:

- 1/2 pound ground beef or chicken
- 1 onion, finely chopped
- 2 cloves garlic, minced
- 1 teaspoon ground cumin
- 1 teaspoon ground coriander
- 1/2 teaspoon ground turmeric
- 1/2 teaspoon chili powder (optional)
- Salt and black pepper, to taste
- Chopped fresh cilantro or parsley, for garnish

Instructions:

1. In a large mixing bowl, combine the all-purpose flour and salt. Gradually add the warm water, stirring continuously, until a soft dough forms. Knead the dough for a few minutes until smooth and elastic. Cover the bowl with a clean kitchen towel and let it rest for about 30 minutes.
2. While the dough is resting, prepare the filling. In a skillet, heat a little vegetable oil over medium heat. Add the chopped onion and minced garlic, and sauté until softened and fragrant.
3. Add the ground beef or chicken to the skillet and cook until browned, breaking it up with a spoon as it cooks.
4. Stir in the ground cumin, ground coriander, ground turmeric, chili powder (if using), salt, and black pepper. Cook for another few minutes until the spices are fragrant and well combined with the meat mixture. Remove from heat and let it cool slightly.
5. Divide the dough into equal-sized balls. Roll out each ball into a thin circle on a lightly floured surface.

6. Spoon a portion of the meat filling onto one half of each dough circle, leaving a small border around the edges.
7. Fold the other half of the dough over the filling to enclose it, pressing the edges together to seal.
8. Heat a little vegetable oil in a skillet over medium heat. Carefully transfer the stuffed dough to the skillet and cook until golden brown and crispy on both sides, flipping halfway through. Repeat with the remaining dough and filling.
9. Once cooked, transfer the Mutabbaq to a serving platter and garnish with chopped fresh cilantro or parsley.
10. Serve the Mutabbaq hot, accompanied by a tangy dipping sauce or a side of pickled vegetables.

Enjoy the crispy and flavorful Mutabbaq as a delicious snack or appetizer, and savor the savory filling wrapped in golden-brown dough. Adjust the spices and fillings according to your taste preferences.

Kanafeh

Ingredients:

- 1 package (16 ounces) shredded phyllo dough (kataifi), thawed if frozen
- 1 cup unsalted butter, melted
- 2 cups finely ground unsalted pistachios or walnuts
- 2 cups shredded mozzarella cheese (or any soft white cheese, such as Akkawi or Nabulsi)
- 1 cup granulated sugar
- 1 cup water
- 1 tablespoon rose water or orange blossom water
- Chopped pistachios or almonds, for garnish
- Powdered sugar, for dusting

Instructions:

1. Preheat your oven to 350°F (175°C). Lightly grease a 9x13-inch baking dish with butter or cooking spray.
2. In a large bowl, gently separate the strands of shredded phyllo dough with your fingers, breaking up any clumps.
3. Pour the melted butter over the shredded phyllo dough and toss until evenly coated.
4. Press half of the buttered phyllo dough mixture into the bottom of the prepared baking dish, pressing down firmly to form an even layer.
5. Sprinkle the finely ground nuts evenly over the layer of phyllo dough.
6. Spread the shredded cheese evenly over the layer of nuts, pressing down gently.
7. Cover the cheese layer with the remaining buttered phyllo dough mixture, pressing down firmly to form another even layer.
8. Bake in the preheated oven for 30-35 minutes, or until the top is golden brown and crispy.
9. While the Kanafeh is baking, prepare the syrup. In a saucepan, combine the granulated sugar and water. Bring to a boil over medium heat, stirring until the sugar has dissolved.
10. Reduce the heat to low and simmer for 10-15 minutes, or until the syrup has thickened slightly. Remove from heat and stir in the rose water or orange blossom water. Let the syrup cool slightly.
11. Once the Kanafeh is done baking, remove it from the oven and immediately pour the warm syrup evenly over the hot pastry.

12. Allow the Kanafeh to cool for at least 10-15 minutes before slicing into squares or wedges.
13. Garnish the Kanafeh with chopped pistachios or almonds and a dusting of powdered sugar before serving.

Enjoy the rich and indulgent flavors of homemade Kanafeh as a delightful dessert, and savor the contrast of textures between the crispy pastry, gooey cheese, and sweet syrup. Adjust the filling and syrup according to your taste preferences.

Basbousa

Ingredients:

For the cake:

- 1 cup semolina flour
- 1 cup granulated sugar
- 1 cup plain yogurt
- 1/2 cup unsweetened desiccated coconut
- 1/2 cup unsalted butter, melted
- 1 teaspoon baking powder
- 1/4 teaspoon baking soda
- 1/4 teaspoon salt
- 1 teaspoon vanilla extract
- Sliced almonds or whole blanched almonds, for garnish

For the syrup:

- 1 cup granulated sugar
- 1 cup water
- 1 tablespoon lemon juice
- 1 tablespoon rose water or orange blossom water (optional)

Instructions:

1. Preheat your oven to 350°F (175°C). Grease a 9x9-inch baking dish with butter or cooking spray.
2. In a large mixing bowl, combine the semolina flour, sugar, desiccated coconut, baking powder, baking soda, and salt.
3. Add the melted butter, plain yogurt, and vanilla extract to the dry ingredients. Mix until well combined and a thick batter forms.
4. Transfer the batter to the prepared baking dish and spread it out evenly using a spatula or the back of a spoon.
5. Use a sharp knife to score the surface of the batter into diamond-shaped or square pieces. Press a sliced almond or whole blanched almond into the center of each piece.
6. Bake in the preheated oven for 30-35 minutes, or until the top is golden brown and a toothpick inserted into the center comes out clean.

7. While the Basbousa is baking, prepare the syrup. In a saucepan, combine the granulated sugar, water, and lemon juice. Bring to a boil over medium heat, stirring until the sugar has dissolved.
8. Reduce the heat to low and simmer the syrup for 10-15 minutes, or until it has thickened slightly. Stir in the rose water or orange blossom water, if using, and remove from heat.
9. Once the Basbousa is done baking, remove it from the oven and immediately pour the warm syrup evenly over the hot cake.
10. Let the Basbousa cool in the baking dish for at least 30 minutes before slicing and serving.

Enjoy the sweet and aromatic flavors of homemade Basbousa as a delightful dessert or snack, and savor the moist and tender texture with every bite. Store any leftovers in an airtight container at room temperature for up to 3 days.

Maamoul

Ingredients:

For the dough:

- 3 cups all-purpose flour
- 1 cup unsalted butter, softened
- 1/2 cup powdered sugar
- 1/4 cup milk or water
- 1 teaspoon rose water or orange blossom water (optional)

For the date filling:

- 2 cups pitted dates
- 1 tablespoon unsalted butter
- 1 teaspoon ground cinnamon
- 1/4 teaspoon ground nutmeg
- 1/4 teaspoon ground cloves
- 1 tablespoon orange blossom water (optional)

Instructions:

1. To prepare the date filling, place the pitted dates in a saucepan with enough water to cover them. Bring to a boil over medium heat, then reduce the heat to low and simmer for about 10-15 minutes, or until the dates are soft and mushy.
2. Remove the dates from the heat and drain any excess water. Mash the softened dates with a fork or potato masher until smooth.
3. Add the unsalted butter, ground cinnamon, ground nutmeg, ground cloves, and orange blossom water (if using) to the mashed dates. Stir until well combined. Set aside to cool.
4. In a large mixing bowl, cream together the softened unsalted butter and powdered sugar until light and fluffy.
5. Gradually add the all-purpose flour to the butter mixture, mixing until a soft dough forms. If the dough is too dry, add the milk or water, one tablespoon at a time, until the dough comes together.
6. Divide the dough into small balls, about the size of a walnut.

7. To shape the Maamoul, flatten each dough ball in the palm of your hand to form a small disc. Place a teaspoon of the date filling in the center of the disc.
8. Enclose the date filling by folding the edges of the dough over it, then roll it between your palms to form a smooth ball. Press the ball into a Maamoul mold or use your fingers to create decorative patterns on the surface.
9. Arrange the shaped Maamoul on a baking sheet lined with parchment paper, leaving some space between each pastry.
10. Preheat your oven to 350°F (175°C). Bake the Maamoul in the preheated oven for 15-20 minutes, or until they are golden brown on the bottom.
11. Remove the Maamoul from the oven and let them cool on the baking sheet for a few minutes before transferring them to a wire rack to cool completely.

Enjoy the sweet and fragrant flavors of homemade Maamoul with date filling as a delightful treat during special occasions or as a snack with a cup of tea or coffee. Store any leftovers in an airtight container at room temperature for up to one week.

Khubz (Flatbread)

Ingredients:

- 4 cups all-purpose flour
- 1 teaspoon salt
- 2 teaspoons active dry yeast
- 1 teaspoon granulated sugar
- 1 1/2 cups warm water
- 2 tablespoons olive oil, plus extra for brushing

Instructions:

1. In a small bowl, combine the warm water, active dry yeast, and granulated sugar. Stir gently and let it sit for about 5-10 minutes, or until the mixture becomes frothy.
2. In a large mixing bowl, combine the all-purpose flour and salt. Make a well in the center of the flour mixture and pour in the activated yeast mixture and olive oil.
3. Use a wooden spoon or your hands to mix the ingredients together until a rough dough forms.
4. Transfer the dough to a floured surface and knead it for about 8-10 minutes, or until it becomes smooth and elastic. Add more flour if the dough is too sticky.
5. Shape the dough into a ball and place it in a lightly greased bowl. Cover the bowl with a clean kitchen towel or plastic wrap and let the dough rise in a warm, draft-free place for about 1-2 hours, or until it doubles in size.
6. Once the dough has risen, punch it down to release the air bubbles and divide it into equal-sized balls.
7. Preheat your oven to the highest temperature setting, typically around 500°F (260°C), and place a baking stone or overturned baking sheet in the oven to heat up.
8. Roll out each dough ball into a circle or oval shape, about 1/4 inch thick. You can use a rolling pin or your hands to flatten the dough.
9. Carefully transfer the rolled-out dough to the hot baking stone or baking sheet in the oven. Cook for about 2-3 minutes on each side, or until the bread puffs up and develops golden brown spots.
10. Remove the Khubz from the oven and brush each bread with a little olive oil for added flavor and shine.
11. Serve the Khubz warm with your favorite Middle Eastern dishes or use it to make wraps or sandwiches.

Enjoy the delicious and versatile Khubz as a perfect accompaniment to your favorite Middle Eastern meals, or use it as a base for wraps, sandwiches, or even pizza. Customize the flavor by adding herbs, spices, or seeds to the dough before baking. Store any leftovers in an airtight container or resealable plastic bag at room temperature for up to a few days.

Balaleet

Ingredients:

- 1 cup vermicelli noodles
- 4 eggs
- 1 tablespoon butter or ghee
- 1/4 cup granulated sugar (adjust to taste)
- 1/4 teaspoon ground cardamom (optional)
- Pinch of saffron threads (optional)
- Salt, to taste
- Chopped nuts (such as almonds or pistachios), for garnish
- Raisins, for garnish

Instructions:

1. Start by cooking the vermicelli noodles according to the package instructions. Drain the noodles and set them aside.
2. In a small bowl, soak the saffron threads in a tablespoon of warm water for a few minutes to release their flavor and color. Set aside.
3. In a large skillet or frying pan, melt the butter or ghee over medium heat.
4. Add the cooked vermicelli noodles to the skillet and sauté them for a few minutes until they start to turn golden brown and crispy.
5. In a separate bowl, beat the eggs with the granulated sugar, ground cardamom (if using), and a pinch of salt until well combined.
6. Pour the egg mixture over the sautéed vermicelli noodles in the skillet. Stir gently to combine, ensuring that the eggs are evenly distributed.
7. Cook the mixture over medium heat, stirring occasionally, until the eggs are fully cooked and set.
8. Once the eggs are cooked, drizzle the saffron water over the Balaleet and give it a gentle stir to distribute the saffron flavor and color.
9. Transfer the Balaleet to a serving platter or individual plates.
10. Garnish the Balaleet with chopped nuts (such as almonds or pistachios) and raisins before serving.

Enjoy the comforting and flavorful Balaleet as a unique breakfast dish or as a sweet treat any time of the day. Adjust the sweetness according to your taste preferences by adding more or less sugar. You can also experiment with different garnishes such as shredded coconut or dried fruits.

Harees Laham

Ingredients:

- 1 cup whole wheat grains
- 1 pound lamb or chicken, cut into small pieces
- 1 onion, finely chopped
- 4 cloves garlic, minced
- 1 teaspoon ground cumin
- 1 teaspoon ground coriander
- 1/2 teaspoon ground cinnamon
- 1/4 teaspoon ground cardamom
- Salt and black pepper, to taste
- Water, as needed
- Olive oil, for drizzling (optional)
- Chopped fresh parsley or cilantro, for garnish

Instructions:

1. Rinse the whole wheat grains under cold water until the water runs clear. Drain and set aside.
2. In a large pot or Dutch oven, heat a little olive oil over medium heat. Add the chopped onion and minced garlic, and sauté until softened and fragrant.
3. Add the pieces of lamb or chicken to the pot and cook until browned on all sides.
4. Stir in the ground cumin, ground coriander, ground cinnamon, ground cardamom, salt, and black pepper. Cook for a few minutes until the spices are fragrant.
5. Add the rinsed whole wheat grains to the pot and stir to combine with the meat and spices.
6. Pour enough water into the pot to cover the meat and wheat mixture by about 2 inches.
7. Bring the mixture to a boil over medium-high heat, then reduce the heat to low and let it simmer, covered, for about 2-3 hours, stirring occasionally. Add more water if needed to prevent the mixture from sticking to the bottom of the pot and burning.
8. Continue to cook the Harees over low heat until the meat is tender and the wheat grains have softened and broken down into a smooth and creamy consistency. This can take several hours, so be patient and keep an eye on the pot, adding more water as needed.

9. Once the Harees Laham is cooked to your desired consistency, remove it from the heat and let it cool slightly.
10. Serve the Harees Laham warm, drizzled with a little olive oil if desired, and garnished with chopped fresh parsley or cilantro.

Enjoy the rich and comforting flavors of homemade Harees Laham as a satisfying meal during Ramadan or any time of the year. You can adjust the seasoning and spices according to your taste preferences. Leftovers can be stored in the refrigerator for up to 3-4 days or frozen for longer-term storage. Simply reheat before serving.

Ful Medames

Ingredients:

- 2 cups dried fava beans
- 4 cups water
- 4 cloves garlic, minced
- 1/4 cup olive oil
- Juice of 1 lemon
- 1 teaspoon ground cumin
- 1 teaspoon ground coriander
- Salt, to taste
- Fresh parsley or cilantro, chopped, for garnish
- Optional toppings: diced tomatoes, chopped onions, pickled vegetables, hard-boiled eggs

Instructions:

1. Rinse the dried fava beans under cold water, then place them in a large bowl and cover with water. Let them soak overnight, or for at least 8 hours.
2. Drain the soaked fava beans and rinse them again. Transfer them to a large pot and cover with fresh water.
3. Bring the pot to a boil over medium-high heat, then reduce the heat to low and simmer, partially covered, for 1 to 1.5 hours, or until the beans are tender. Add more water if needed to keep the beans submerged.
4. Once the beans are cooked, remove them from the heat and drain any excess water.
5. In a separate skillet, heat the olive oil over medium heat. Add the minced garlic and cook until fragrant, about 1 minute.
6. Add the cooked fava beans to the skillet with the garlic, along with the ground cumin, ground coriander, and salt. Stir to combine and cook for another 5-10 minutes, mashing some of the beans with the back of a spoon or a potato masher to thicken the mixture slightly.
7. Remove the skillet from the heat and stir in the lemon juice.
8. Transfer the Ful Medames to a serving dish and garnish with chopped fresh parsley or cilantro.
9. Serve the Ful Medames warm, accompanied by pita bread or other flatbread. Optionally, you can top it with diced tomatoes, chopped onions, pickled vegetables, or hard-boiled eggs for extra flavor and texture.

Enjoy the flavorful and nutritious Ful Medames for breakfast, brunch, or as a satisfying snack. It's a versatile dish that can be customized with your favorite toppings and spices. Adjust the seasoning according to your taste preferences. Leftovers can be stored in the refrigerator for up to 3-4 days and reheated before serving.

Luqaimat

Ingredients:

- 2 cups all-purpose flour
- 1 teaspoon instant yeast
- 1 tablespoon sugar
- 1/2 teaspoon salt
- 1 cup warm water
- Vegetable oil, for frying
- Date syrup, honey, or sugar syrup, for drizzling
- Sesame seeds or powdered sugar, for garnish (optional)

Instructions:

1. In a large mixing bowl, combine the all-purpose flour, instant yeast, sugar, and salt.
2. Gradually add the warm water to the dry ingredients, stirring continuously, until a smooth and slightly sticky dough forms.
3. Cover the bowl with a clean kitchen towel or plastic wrap and let the dough rest in a warm, draft-free place for about 1-2 hours, or until it doubles in size.
4. Once the dough has risen, heat vegetable oil in a deep frying pan or pot over medium heat until it reaches about 350°F (175°C).
5. Using wet hands or a spoon, scoop out small portions of the dough and shape them into small balls, about the size of a walnut.
6. Carefully drop the dough balls into the hot oil, making sure not to overcrowd the pan. Fry in batches if necessary.
7. Fry the dough balls for about 5-7 minutes, or until they are golden brown and crispy on the outside, and cooked through on the inside. Use a slotted spoon to remove them from the oil and transfer them to a plate lined with paper towels to drain any excess oil.
8. Once all the dough balls are fried, arrange them on a serving platter.
9. Drizzle the Luqaimat with date syrup, honey, or sugar syrup while they are still warm.
10. Optionally, sprinkle sesame seeds or powdered sugar over the Luqaimat for garnish.
11. Serve the Luqaimat immediately while they are still warm and crispy.

Enjoy the delicious and indulgent Luqaimat as a sweet treat during special occasions or as a delightful dessert any time of the year. Adjust the sweetness and flavorings of the syrup according to your taste preferences. These bite-sized delights are sure to be a hit with family and friends.

Jallab

Ingredients:

- 1/2 cup jallab syrup
- 3 cups cold water
- Crushed ice
- Pine nuts, for garnish
- Rose petals, for garnish (optional)

For the Jallab Syrup:

- 1 cup grape molasses
- 1/4 cup rose water
- 1 tablespoon sugar (optional)
- 1/2 teaspoon ground cinnamon
- 1/4 teaspoon ground cloves

Instructions:

1. To make the Jallab syrup, combine the grape molasses, rose water, sugar (if using), ground cinnamon, and ground cloves in a small saucepan.
2. Heat the mixture over medium heat, stirring occasionally, until the sugar has dissolved and the syrup is well combined. Remove from heat and let it cool completely.
3. Once the Jallab syrup has cooled, store it in a sealed container in the refrigerator until ready to use.
4. To prepare the Jallab drink, fill serving glasses with crushed ice.
5. Pour the cold water into a pitcher, then add the Jallab syrup and stir until well combined.
6. Pour the Jallab mixture over the crushed ice in the serving glasses.
7. Garnish each glass with a sprinkle of pine nuts and, if desired, a few rose petals for an extra decorative touch.
8. Serve the Jallab immediately and enjoy its refreshing and sweet flavor.

Adjust the sweetness and flavorings of the Jallab syrup according to your taste preferences. You can also customize the garnishes by adding chopped pistachios, almonds, or raisins. Jallab is best served chilled and enjoyed on a hot day or as a refreshing beverage during Ramadan gatherings and celebrations.

Jareesh Laham

Ingredients:

- 1 cup cracked wheat (bulgur)
- 1 pound lamb or beef, cubed
- 1 onion, finely chopped
- 4 cloves garlic, minced
- 2 tablespoons vegetable oil or clarified butter (ghee)
- 1 teaspoon ground cumin
- 1 teaspoon ground coriander
- 1/2 teaspoon ground cinnamon
- 1/4 teaspoon ground cardamom
- Salt and black pepper, to taste
- Chopped fresh parsley or cilantro, for garnish
- Lemon wedges, for serving

Instructions:

1. Rinse the cracked wheat under cold water, then place it in a bowl and cover with water. Let it soak for about 30 minutes, then drain and set aside.
2. In a large pot or Dutch oven, heat the vegetable oil or clarified butter over medium heat. Add the chopped onion and minced garlic, and sauté until softened and translucent.
3. Add the cubed lamb or beef to the pot and cook until browned on all sides.
4. Stir in the ground cumin, ground coriander, ground cinnamon, ground cardamom, salt, and black pepper. Cook for a few minutes until the spices are fragrant.
5. Add the soaked cracked wheat to the pot and stir to combine with the meat and spices.
6. Pour enough water into the pot to cover the meat and cracked wheat by about 1 inch.
7. Bring the mixture to a boil, then reduce the heat to low and let it simmer, covered, for about 1 to 1.5 hours, or until the meat is tender and the cracked wheat is cooked through, stirring occasionally.
8. Once the Jareesh Laham is cooked, remove it from the heat and let it sit for a few minutes to thicken.
9. Serve the Jareesh Laham hot, garnished with chopped fresh parsley or cilantro, and with lemon wedges on the side for squeezing over the dish.

Enjoy the rich and aromatic flavors of homemade Jareesh Laham as a comforting and satisfying meal. You can adjust the seasoning and spices according to your taste preferences. Leftovers can be stored in the refrigerator for up to 3-4 days and reheated before serving.

Jareesh Dajaj

Ingredients:

- 1 cup cracked wheat (Jareesh)
- 1 pound chicken pieces (with bone-in for added flavor)
- 1 onion, finely chopped
- 2 carrots, diced
- 2 tomatoes, diced
- 3 cloves garlic, minced
- 2 tablespoons vegetable oil or olive oil
- 1 teaspoon ground cumin
- 1 teaspoon ground coriander
- 1/2 teaspoon ground cinnamon
- 1/4 teaspoon ground cardamom
- Salt and black pepper, to taste
- Chopped fresh parsley or cilantro, for garnish
- Lemon wedges, for serving

Instructions:

1. Rinse the cracked wheat under cold water, then place it in a bowl and cover with water. Let it soak for about 30 minutes, then drain and set aside.
2. In a large pot or Dutch oven, heat the vegetable oil over medium heat. Add the chopped onion and minced garlic, and sauté until softened and translucent.
3. Add the chicken pieces to the pot and cook until browned on all sides.
4. Stir in the ground cumin, ground coriander, ground cinnamon, ground cardamom, salt, and black pepper. Cook for a few minutes until the spices are fragrant.
5. Add the soaked cracked wheat to the pot and stir to combine with the chicken and spices.
6. Pour enough water into the pot to cover the chicken and cracked wheat by about 1 inch.
7. Add the diced carrots and tomatoes to the pot and stir to combine.
8. Bring the mixture to a boil, then reduce the heat to low and let it simmer, covered, for about 1 to 1.5 hours, or until the chicken is tender and the cracked wheat is cooked through, stirring occasionally.
9. Once the Jareesh Dajaj is cooked, remove it from the heat and let it sit for a few minutes to thicken.

10. Serve the Jareesh Dajaj hot, garnished with chopped fresh parsley or cilantro, and with lemon wedges on the side for squeezing over the dish.

Enjoy the rich and flavorful Jareesh Dajaj as a comforting and satisfying meal. You can adjust the seasoning and spices according to your taste preferences. Leftovers can be stored in the refrigerator for up to 3-4 days and reheated before serving.

Martabak

Ingredients:

- 2 cups all-purpose flour
- 1 teaspoon salt
- 1 teaspoon sugar
- 1 teaspoon baking powder
- 1 egg
- 1 cup water
- Vegetable oil, for frying

For the filling:

- 1 pound ground beef or chicken
- 1 onion, finely chopped
- 2 cloves garlic, minced
- 1 teaspoon ground cumin
- 1 teaspoon ground coriander
- 1/2 teaspoon turmeric powder
- Salt and black pepper, to taste
- Chopped fresh cilantro or parsley, for garnish

Instructions:

1. In a large mixing bowl, combine the all-purpose flour, salt, sugar, and baking powder. Make a well in the center and add the egg and water. Whisk until smooth and well combined to form a pancake batter. Let it rest for about 30 minutes.
2. In the meantime, prepare the filling. Heat a little vegetable oil in a skillet over medium heat. Add the chopped onion and minced garlic, and sauté until softened and fragrant.
3. Add the ground beef or chicken to the skillet and cook until browned, breaking it up with a spoon as it cooks.
4. Stir in the ground cumin, ground coriander, turmeric powder, salt, and black pepper. Cook for a few more minutes until the spices are fragrant and the meat is cooked through. Remove from heat and let it cool slightly.
5. Heat a non-stick skillet or frying pan over medium heat. Lightly grease the pan with vegetable oil.

6. Pour a ladleful of the pancake batter into the skillet and spread it out evenly to form a thin pancake.
7. Cook the pancake for about 2-3 minutes, or until the bottom is set and lightly golden brown.
8. Spoon a portion of the cooked meat filling onto one half of the pancake.
9. Fold the other half of the pancake over the filling to enclose it, forming a half-moon shape. Press down gently to seal the edges.
10. Cook the Martabak for another 2-3 minutes on each side, or until crispy and golden brown.
11. Repeat the process with the remaining batter and filling.
12. Once cooked, transfer the Martabak to a cutting board and slice into wedges.
13. Serve the Martabak hot, garnished with chopped fresh cilantro or parsley, and with your favorite dipping sauce or pickled vegetables on the side.

Enjoy the delicious and flavorful Martabak as a satisfying snack or meal. You can customize the filling with your favorite ingredients, such as cheese, vegetables, or seafood, to suit your taste preferences.

Samboosa Laham

Ingredients:

For the filling:

- 1 pound ground beef or lamb
- 1 onion, finely chopped
- 2 cloves garlic, minced
- 1 teaspoon ground cumin
- 1 teaspoon ground coriander
- 1/2 teaspoon ground turmeric
- 1/2 teaspoon ground cinnamon
- 1/4 teaspoon cayenne pepper (optional, for heat)
- Salt and black pepper, to taste
- Vegetable oil, for cooking

For the pastry:

- 2 cups all-purpose flour
- 1/2 teaspoon salt
- 1/4 cup vegetable oil
- 1/2 cup warm water

Instructions:

For the filling:

1. Heat a little vegetable oil in a skillet over medium heat. Add the chopped onion and minced garlic, and sauté until softened and translucent.
2. Add the ground beef or lamb to the skillet and cook until browned, breaking it up with a spoon as it cooks.
3. Stir in the ground cumin, ground coriander, ground turmeric, ground cinnamon, cayenne pepper (if using), salt, and black pepper. Cook for a few more minutes until the spices are fragrant and the meat is cooked through. Remove from heat and let it cool slightly.

For the pastry:

1. In a large mixing bowl, combine the all-purpose flour and salt. Add the vegetable oil and mix until the flour resembles coarse crumbs.
2. Gradually add the warm water to the flour mixture, kneading until a smooth dough forms. Cover the dough with a damp cloth and let it rest for about 30 minutes.
3. After resting, divide the dough into small balls, about the size of golf balls. Roll each ball into a thin circle on a floured surface.
4. Cut each circle in half to form semi-circles.
5. Place a spoonful of the meat filling in the center of each semi-circle.
6. Fold one corner of the pastry over the filling to form a triangle, then continue folding along the edges until the filling is completely enclosed. Press the edges firmly to seal.
7. Repeat the process with the remaining dough and filling.

Cooking the samosas:

1. Heat vegetable oil in a deep frying pan or skillet over medium heat.
2. Carefully place the samosas in the hot oil, a few at a time, and fry until golden brown and crispy on all sides, turning occasionally.
3. Once cooked, remove the samosas from the oil and drain on paper towels to remove excess oil.
4. Serve the Samboosa Laham hot, with your favorite dipping sauce or chutney on the side.

Enjoy the delicious and crispy Samboosa Laham as a delightful appetizer or snack. You can customize the filling with your favorite spices and ingredients, such as potatoes, peas, or paneer, to suit your taste preferences.

Dawood Basha

Ingredients:

For the meatballs:

- 1 pound ground beef or lamb
- 1 onion, finely chopped
- 2 cloves garlic, minced
- 1/4 cup chopped fresh parsley
- 1 teaspoon ground cumin
- 1 teaspoon ground coriander
- 1/2 teaspoon cinnamon
- Salt and black pepper, to taste
- 1 egg, beaten
- 1/4 cup breadcrumbs (optional, for binding)

For the tomato sauce:

- 2 tablespoons olive oil
- 1 onion, finely chopped
- 2 cloves garlic, minced
- 1 can (14 oz) crushed tomatoes
- 1 tablespoon tomato paste
- 1 teaspoon ground cumin
- 1 teaspoon ground coriander
- 1/2 teaspoon cinnamon
- Salt and black pepper, to taste
- 1 cup beef or vegetable broth
- Chopped fresh parsley, for garnish (optional)

Instructions:

For the meatballs:

1. In a large mixing bowl, combine the ground beef or lamb, chopped onion, minced garlic, chopped parsley, ground cumin, ground coriander, cinnamon, salt, black pepper, beaten egg, and breadcrumbs (if using). Mix well until all the ingredients are evenly combined.

2. Shape the meat mixture into small meatballs, about 1 inch in diameter, and place them on a baking sheet lined with parchment paper.
3. Preheat the oven to 375°F (190°C). Bake the meatballs in the preheated oven for about 15-20 minutes, or until they are cooked through and lightly browned. Remove from the oven and set aside.

For the tomato sauce:

1. In a large skillet or saucepan, heat the olive oil over medium heat. Add the chopped onion and minced garlic, and sauté until softened and translucent.
2. Add the crushed tomatoes, tomato paste, ground cumin, ground coriander, cinnamon, salt, and black pepper to the skillet. Stir to combine.
3. Pour in the beef or vegetable broth and bring the sauce to a simmer.
4. Once the sauce is simmering, add the baked meatballs to the skillet, gently stirring to coat them in the sauce.
5. Cover the skillet and let the meatballs simmer in the sauce for about 10-15 minutes, allowing the flavors to meld together and the sauce to thicken slightly.
6. Once the meatballs are heated through and the sauce has thickened to your desired consistency, remove the skillet from the heat.
7. Serve the Dawood Basha hot, garnished with chopped fresh parsley if desired. Enjoy the meatballs and sauce with rice, bulgur, or pita bread.

Dawood Basha is a comforting and flavorful dish that is sure to be a hit with family and friends. Adjust the seasoning and spices according to your taste preferences. Leftovers can be stored in the refrigerator for up to 3-4 days and reheated before serving.

Shish Tawook

Ingredients:

- 1.5 pounds boneless, skinless chicken breasts, cut into cubes
- 1/2 cup plain yogurt
- 3 tablespoons lemon juice
- 3 cloves garlic, minced
- 2 tablespoons olive oil
- 1 teaspoon paprika
- 1 teaspoon ground cumin
- 1/2 teaspoon ground coriander
- 1/2 teaspoon ground cinnamon
- 1/4 teaspoon cayenne pepper (optional, for heat)
- Salt and black pepper, to taste
- Wooden or metal skewers, soaked in water (if using wooden skewers)

Instructions:

1. In a large mixing bowl, combine the plain yogurt, lemon juice, minced garlic, olive oil, paprika, ground cumin, ground coriander, ground cinnamon, cayenne pepper (if using), salt, and black pepper. Mix well until the marinade is smooth and well combined.
2. Add the cubed chicken breasts to the marinade, making sure they are evenly coated. Cover the bowl with plastic wrap or a lid and refrigerate for at least 2 hours, or preferably overnight, to allow the flavors to meld and the chicken to marinate thoroughly.
3. If using wooden skewers, soak them in water for at least 30 minutes to prevent them from burning during grilling.
4. Preheat the grill to medium-high heat. If using a charcoal grill, prepare the charcoal and let it heat until it reaches medium-high temperature.
5. Thread the marinated chicken cubes onto the skewers, leaving a small space between each piece to ensure even cooking.
6. Brush the grill grates with a little oil to prevent sticking, then place the chicken skewers on the grill.
7. Grill the Shish Tawook for about 8-10 minutes, turning occasionally, or until the chicken is cooked through and has charred grill marks on all sides.
8. Once cooked, remove the chicken skewers from the grill and transfer them to a serving platter.

9. Serve the Shish Tawook hot, garnished with chopped fresh parsley or cilantro, and with your favorite accompaniments such as grilled vegetables, rice, or pita bread.

Enjoy the tender and flavorful Shish Tawook chicken kebabs as a delicious main dish or appetizer. They are perfect for grilling outdoors during summer gatherings or indoor cooking year-round. Adjust the seasoning and spices according to your taste preferences. Leftover marinated chicken can be stored in the refrigerator for up to 2 days before grilling.

Molokhia

Ingredients:

- 2 cups fresh or frozen Molokhia leaves (Jew's mallow)
- 4 cups chicken or vegetable broth
- 1 onion, finely chopped
- 4 cloves garlic, minced
- 2 tablespoons olive oil
- Salt and black pepper, to taste
- Lemon wedges, for serving
- Cooked rice or flatbread, for serving (optional)

Instructions:

1. If using fresh Molokhia leaves, wash them thoroughly under cold water to remove any dirt or debris. If using frozen Molokhia leaves, thaw them according to the package instructions.
2. Heat the olive oil in a large pot or Dutch oven over medium heat. Add the chopped onion and minced garlic, and sauté until softened and fragrant.
3. Add the Molokhia leaves to the pot and stir to combine with the onions and garlic.
4. Pour the chicken or vegetable broth into the pot, ensuring that the Molokhia leaves are fully submerged in the liquid. Bring the mixture to a simmer.
5. Let the Molokhia soup simmer gently for about 15-20 minutes, stirring occasionally, until the leaves are tender and wilted.
6. Season the soup with salt and black pepper to taste, adjusting the seasoning as needed.
7. Once the Molokhia leaves are fully cooked and the flavors have melded together, remove the pot from the heat.
8. Serve the Molokhia soup hot, with lemon wedges on the side for squeezing over the soup. You can also serve the soup with cooked rice or flatbread on the side for a more substantial meal.

Enjoy the comforting and nutritious Molokhia soup as a satisfying meal on its own or as a starter to a Middle Eastern feast. Feel free to customize the soup by adding other vegetables, herbs, or spices according to your taste preferences.

Mutabbaq Laham

Ingredients:

For the pancake dough:

- 2 cups all-purpose flour
- 1 teaspoon salt
- 1 cup water
- 2 tablespoons vegetable oil

For the meat filling:

- 1 pound ground beef or lamb
- 1 onion, finely chopped
- 2 cloves garlic, minced
- 1 teaspoon ground cumin
- 1 teaspoon ground coriander
- 1/2 teaspoon ground turmeric
- 1/2 teaspoon paprika
- Salt and black pepper, to taste
- Vegetable oil, for cooking

Instructions:

For the pancake dough:

1. In a large mixing bowl, combine the all-purpose flour and salt. Gradually add the water, mixing until a smooth dough forms.
2. Knead the dough on a lightly floured surface for a few minutes until it becomes elastic and smooth. Shape the dough into a ball and cover it with a damp cloth. Let it rest for about 30 minutes.

For the meat filling:

1. In a skillet or frying pan, heat a little vegetable oil over medium heat. Add the chopped onion and minced garlic, and sauté until softened and translucent.
2. Add the ground beef or lamb to the skillet and cook until browned, breaking it up with a spoon as it cooks.
3. Stir in the ground cumin, ground coriander, ground turmeric, paprika, salt, and black pepper. Cook for a few more minutes until the spices are fragrant and the meat is cooked through. Remove from heat and let it cool slightly.

Assembling the Mutabbaq:

1. Divide the rested dough into equal-sized balls, about the size of golf balls.
2. On a lightly floured surface, roll out each ball of dough into a thin circle, about 6-8 inches in diameter.
3. Place a spoonful of the cooked meat filling in the center of each dough circle, spreading it out slightly.
4. Fold the edges of the dough circle over the filling to enclose it completely, forming a square or rectangular shape. Press down gently to seal the edges.
5. Heat a little vegetable oil in a skillet or frying pan over medium heat. Carefully transfer the stuffed pancake to the hot pan and cook for about 3-4 minutes on each side, or until golden brown and crispy.
6. Once cooked, remove the Mutabbaq from the pan and drain on paper towels to remove excess oil.
7. Repeat the process with the remaining dough and filling.

Serve the Mutabbaq Laham hot, sliced into portions, and enjoy the delicious combination of crispy pancake and flavorful meat filling. You can also serve it with your favorite dipping sauce or yogurt on the side for added flavor.

Qursan

Ingredients:

For the flatbread dough:

- 2 cups all-purpose flour
- 1 teaspoon salt
- 3/4 cup warm water
- 2 tablespoons olive oil

For the filling:

- 1 pound ground beef or lamb
- 1 onion, finely chopped
- 2 cloves garlic, minced
- 1 teaspoon ground cumin
- 1 teaspoon ground coriander
- 1/2 teaspoon ground cinnamon
- Salt and black pepper, to taste
- Vegetable oil, for cooking

Instructions:

For the flatbread dough:

1. In a large mixing bowl, combine the all-purpose flour and salt. Gradually add the warm water and olive oil, mixing until a dough forms.
2. Knead the dough on a lightly floured surface for about 5-7 minutes, or until it becomes smooth and elastic. Shape the dough into a ball and cover it with a damp cloth. Let it rest for about 30 minutes.

For the filling:

1. In a skillet or frying pan, heat a little vegetable oil over medium heat. Add the chopped onion and minced garlic, and sauté until softened and translucent.

2. Add the ground beef or lamb to the skillet and cook until browned, breaking it up with a spoon as it cooks.
3. Stir in the ground cumin, ground coriander, ground cinnamon, salt, and black pepper. Cook for a few more minutes until the spices are fragrant and the meat is cooked through. Remove from heat and let it cool slightly.

Assembling the Qursan:

1. Preheat the oven to 350°F (175°C).
2. Divide the rested dough into equal-sized balls, about the size of golf balls.
3. On a lightly floured surface, roll out each ball of dough into a thin circle, about 8-10 inches in diameter.
4. Place a spoonful of the cooked meat filling in the center of each dough circle, spreading it out slightly.
5. Fold the edges of the dough circle over the filling to enclose it completely, forming a square or rectangular shape. Press down gently to seal the edges.
6. Place the stuffed flatbreads on a baking sheet lined with parchment paper.
7. Bake the Qursan in the preheated oven for about 15-20 minutes, or until the bread is crispy and golden brown.
8. Once cooked, remove the Qursan from the oven and let them cool slightly before serving.

Serve the Qursan hot, sliced into portions, and enjoy the delicious combination of crispy flatbread and flavorful meat filling. You can also serve it with your favorite dipping sauce or yogurt on the side for added flavor.

Kabsa Dajaj

Ingredients:

For the chicken marinade:

- 2 pounds chicken pieces (legs, thighs, or breasts)
- 1/4 cup yogurt
- 2 tablespoons tomato paste
- 2 tablespoons lemon juice
- 2 cloves garlic, minced
- 1 teaspoon ground cumin
- 1 teaspoon ground coriander
- 1/2 teaspoon ground turmeric
- 1/2 teaspoon ground cinnamon
- Salt and black pepper, to taste

For the rice:

- 2 cups basmati rice, rinsed and soaked for 30 minutes
- 3 tablespoons vegetable oil or ghee
- 1 onion, finely chopped
- 2 cloves garlic, minced
- 2 tomatoes, diced
- 1 carrot, grated (optional)
- 1 tablespoon tomato paste
- 1 teaspoon ground cumin
- 1 teaspoon ground coriander
- 1/2 teaspoon ground cardamom
- 1/2 teaspoon ground cloves
- 1/2 teaspoon ground cinnamon
- Salt and black pepper, to taste
- 4 cups chicken broth or water
- Chopped fresh cilantro or parsley, for garnish (optional)
- Almonds or pine nuts, toasted, for garnish (optional)

Instructions:

For the chicken marinade:

1. In a large bowl, combine the yogurt, tomato paste, lemon juice, minced garlic, ground cumin, ground coriander, ground turmeric, ground cinnamon, salt, and black pepper. Mix well to combine.
2. Add the chicken pieces to the marinade, making sure they are well coated. Cover the bowl and let the chicken marinate in the refrigerator for at least 1 hour, or preferably overnight, to allow the flavors to meld.

For the rice:

1. In a large pot or Dutch oven, heat the vegetable oil or ghee over medium heat. Add the chopped onion and minced garlic, and sauté until softened and translucent.
2. Add the diced tomatoes and grated carrot (if using) to the pot, and cook for a few minutes until the tomatoes start to soften.
3. Stir in the tomato paste, ground cumin, ground coriander, ground cardamom, ground cloves, ground cinnamon, salt, and black pepper. Cook for another minute until the spices are fragrant.
4. Drain the soaked rice and add it to the pot, stirring to coat the rice with the spice mixture.
5. Arrange the marinated chicken pieces on top of the rice in the pot.
6. Pour the chicken broth or water over the rice and chicken, ensuring that the rice is fully submerged in the liquid.
7. Bring the mixture to a boil, then reduce the heat to low. Cover the pot and let the Kabsa Dajaj simmer gently for about 20-25 minutes, or until the rice is cooked and the chicken is tender.
8. Once cooked, remove the pot from the heat and let it sit, covered, for a few minutes to allow the flavors to meld.
9. Fluff the rice with a fork and transfer it to a serving platter. Arrange the chicken pieces on top of the rice.
10. Garnish the Kabsa Dajaj with chopped fresh cilantro or parsley, and toasted almonds or pine nuts, if desired.
11. Serve the Kabsa Dajaj hot, accompanied by yogurt, salad, or your favorite condiments on the side.

Enjoy the aromatic and flavorful Saudi Arabian Chicken Kabsa as a delicious and satisfying meal for your family and friends! Adjust the spices and seasoning according to your taste preferences.

Harraq Usfur

Ingredients:

- 4-6 whole pigeons, cleaned and rinsed
- 2 onions, finely chopped
- 4 cloves garlic, minced
- 2 tomatoes, diced
- 2 tablespoons tomato paste
- 1 teaspoon ground cumin
- 1 teaspoon ground coriander
- 1/2 teaspoon ground turmeric
- 1/2 teaspoon ground cinnamon
- 1/4 teaspoon ground cloves
- Salt and black pepper, to taste
- Vegetable oil, for cooking
- Water or chicken broth, as needed
- Fresh parsley or cilantro, for garnish (optional)
- Cooked rice or bread, for serving

Instructions:

1. In a large pot or Dutch oven, heat a little vegetable oil over medium heat. Add the chopped onions and minced garlic, and sauté until softened and fragrant.
2. Add the diced tomatoes and tomato paste to the pot, and cook for a few minutes until the tomatoes start to break down.
3. Stir in the ground cumin, ground coriander, ground turmeric, ground cinnamon, ground cloves, salt, and black pepper. Cook for another minute until the spices are fragrant.
4. Add the cleaned and rinsed whole pigeons to the pot, and brown them on all sides for a few minutes.
5. Pour enough water or chicken broth into the pot to cover the pigeons completely. Bring the mixture to a boil, then reduce the heat to low. Cover the pot and let the pigeons simmer gently for about 1-1.5 hours, or until they are tender and cooked through.
6. Once the pigeons are cooked, remove them from the pot and set them aside. Skim off any excess fat or impurities from the surface of the broth, if necessary.
7. If desired, you can strain the broth to remove any solids and return it to the pot.
8. Taste the broth and adjust the seasoning as needed with salt and black pepper.

9. To serve, arrange the cooked pigeons on a serving platter and pour the hot broth over the top. Garnish with chopped fresh parsley or cilantro, if desired.
10. Serve the Harraq Usfur hot, accompanied by cooked rice or bread on the side.

Enjoy the flavorful and comforting Saudi Arabian Pigeon Stew as a hearty meal for special occasions or gatherings with family and friends! Adjust the spices and seasoning according to your taste preferences.

Mathloutha

Ingredients:

- 2 tablespoons vegetable oil
- 1 onion, finely chopped
- 2 cloves garlic, minced
- 2 carrots, peeled and diced
- 2 potatoes, peeled and diced
- 1 cup green beans, trimmed and cut into bite-sized pieces
- 1 cup cauliflower florets
- 1 cup canned chickpeas, drained and rinsed
- 1 cup canned diced tomatoes
- 4 cups vegetable broth or water
- 1 teaspoon ground cumin
- 1 teaspoon ground coriander
- 1/2 teaspoon ground turmeric
- Salt and black pepper, to taste
- Chopped fresh parsley or cilantro, for garnish (optional)
- Cooked rice or bread, for serving

Instructions:

1. In a large pot or Dutch oven, heat the vegetable oil over medium heat. Add the chopped onion and minced garlic, and sauté until softened and fragrant.
2. Add the diced carrots and potatoes to the pot, and cook for a few minutes until they start to soften.
3. Stir in the green beans, cauliflower florets, canned chickpeas, and diced tomatoes. Cook for another minute, stirring to combine.
4. Pour the vegetable broth or water into the pot, ensuring that the vegetables are fully submerged in the liquid.
5. Add the ground cumin, ground coriander, ground turmeric, salt, and black pepper to the pot, and stir to combine.
6. Bring the mixture to a boil, then reduce the heat to low. Cover the pot and let the Mathloutha simmer gently for about 20-25 minutes, or until the vegetables are tender and cooked through.
7. Taste the stew and adjust the seasoning as needed with salt and black pepper.
8. To serve, ladle the Mathloutha into bowls and garnish with chopped fresh parsley or cilantro, if desired.

9. Serve the Mathloutha hot, accompanied by cooked rice or bread on the side.

Enjoy the wholesome and comforting Saudi Arabian Vegetable Stew as a delicious and satisfying meal for your family and friends! You can customize the stew by adding other vegetables or legumes of your choice, as well as spices and herbs according to your taste preferences.

Biryani

Ingredients:

For the marinade:

- 2 pounds chicken, cut into pieces
- 1 cup plain yogurt
- 2 tablespoons ginger-garlic paste
- 1 teaspoon ground turmeric
- 1 teaspoon red chili powder
- 1 teaspoon ground cumin
- 1 teaspoon ground coriander
- Salt, to taste

For the rice:

- 2 cups Basmati rice, soaked for 30 minutes and drained
- 4 cups water
- 2 bay leaves
- 4 green cardamom pods
- 4 whole cloves
- 1-inch cinnamon stick
- Salt, to taste

For the biryani:

- 3 tablespoons ghee or vegetable oil
- 2 onions, thinly sliced
- 2 tomatoes, chopped
- 2 green chilies, slit lengthwise
- 1/2 cup chopped fresh cilantro (coriander leaves)
- 1/2 cup chopped fresh mint leaves
- 1 teaspoon garam masala
- Saffron strands, soaked in warm milk (optional)

Instructions:

Marinating the chicken:

1. In a large bowl, combine the chicken pieces with yogurt, ginger-garlic paste, ground turmeric, red chili powder, ground cumin, ground coriander, and salt. Mix well to coat the chicken pieces evenly. Cover and refrigerate for at least 1 hour, or preferably overnight, to allow the flavors to meld.

Cooking the rice:

1. In a large pot, bring water to a boil. Add the soaked and drained Basmati rice, bay leaves, green cardamom pods, whole cloves, cinnamon stick, and salt. Cook the rice until it's 70-80% cooked, about 8-10 minutes. Drain the rice and set aside.

Assembling the biryani:

1. In a large heavy-bottomed pot or Dutch oven, heat ghee or vegetable oil over medium heat. Add the sliced onions and cook until they turn golden brown and caramelized. Remove half of the caramelized onions and set aside for garnishing.
2. To the remaining onions in the pot, add the marinated chicken pieces along with any marinade left in the bowl. Cook for about 5-7 minutes until the chicken is partially cooked.
3. Add the chopped tomatoes, green chilies, chopped cilantro, and chopped mint leaves to the pot. Stir well to combine.
4. Spread half of the partially cooked rice evenly over the chicken mixture in the pot.
5. Sprinkle half of the garam masala over the rice layer. Drizzle half of the saffron-infused milk (if using) over the rice.
6. Layer the remaining rice over the first layer and sprinkle the remaining garam masala on top. Drizzle the remaining saffron-infused milk over the rice.
7. Cover the pot with a tight-fitting lid and cook over low heat for about 20-25 minutes, or until the chicken is cooked through and the rice is fully cooked and fluffy.
8. Once done, remove the pot from the heat and let it sit, covered, for a few minutes.
9. Gently fluff the biryani with a fork, being careful not to break the rice grains.
10. Garnish the biryani with the reserved caramelized onions and additional chopped cilantro and mint leaves, if desired.
11. Serve the Chicken Biryani hot with raita (yogurt dip), pickle, and salad on the side.

Enjoy the aromatic and flavorful Chicken Biryani as a delicious and satisfying meal for your family and friends! Adjust the spices and seasoning according to your taste preferences. Biryani pairs well with a variety of accompaniments, such as cucumber raita, mint chutney, or a simple salad.

Kleeja Tamr

Ingredients:

For the dough:

- 3 cups all-purpose flour
- 1 cup unsalted butter, softened
- 1/2 cup powdered sugar
- 1/4 cup milk
- 1 teaspoon vanilla extract
- Pinch of salt

For the date filling:

- 2 cups pitted dates, chopped
- 1/4 cup water
- 1/2 teaspoon ground cardamom
- 1/4 teaspoon ground cinnamon
- 1/4 teaspoon ground cloves
- 1/4 teaspoon ground nutmeg

Instructions:

For the date filling:

1. In a saucepan, combine the chopped dates and water. Cook over medium heat, stirring occasionally, until the dates are soft and the mixture forms a thick paste.
2. Stir in the ground cardamom, ground cinnamon, ground cloves, and ground nutmeg. Cook for another minute to allow the spices to meld with the date mixture. Remove from heat and let it cool completely.

For the dough:

1. In a large mixing bowl, cream together the softened butter and powdered sugar until light and fluffy.

2. Add the milk and vanilla extract to the butter mixture, and mix until well combined.
3. Gradually add the flour and salt to the mixture, mixing until a smooth dough forms. If the dough is too dry, you can add a little more milk, one tablespoon at a time, until it reaches the right consistency.
4. Divide the dough into equal-sized balls, about the size of golf balls.

Assembling the Kleeja Tamr:

1. Preheat the oven to 350°F (175°C) and line a baking sheet with parchment paper.
2. Take one dough ball and flatten it into a circle on a lightly floured surface. Place a spoonful of the date filling in the center of the circle.
3. Fold the edges of the dough over the date filling, pinching them together to seal. You can also use a fork to crimp the edges for a decorative touch.
4. Repeat the process with the remaining dough balls and date filling, placing the filled pastries on the prepared baking sheet.
5. Bake the Kleeja Tamr in the preheated oven for about 15-20 minutes, or until they are golden brown and slightly crisp on the edges.
6. Once baked, remove the Kleeja Tamr from the oven and let them cool on the baking sheet for a few minutes before transferring them to a wire rack to cool completely.

Enjoy the delicious and aromatic Kleeja Tamr with a cup of tea or coffee for a delightful treat! Store any leftover pastries in an airtight container at room temperature for up to several days.

Kleeja Halwa

Ingredients:

- 2 cups pitted dates, chopped
- 1 cup chopped nuts (such as walnuts, almonds, or pistachios)
- 1/4 cup unsalted butter or ghee
- 1/4 cup honey or sugar (adjust to taste)
- 1/4 teaspoon ground cardamom
- 1/4 teaspoon ground cinnamon
- 1/4 teaspoon ground cloves
- 1/4 teaspoon ground nutmeg
- Pinch of salt

Instructions:

1. In a food processor or blender, pulse the chopped dates until they form a thick paste-like consistency. You may need to add a tablespoon or two of water if the dates are too dry.
2. In a large skillet or saucepan, melt the unsalted butter or ghee over medium heat.
3. Add the chopped nuts to the skillet and toast them for a few minutes until they are fragrant and lightly golden brown. Remove the nuts from the skillet and set them aside.
4. To the same skillet, add the date paste, honey or sugar, ground cardamom, ground cinnamon, ground cloves, ground nutmeg, and a pinch of salt. Stir well to combine.
5. Cook the date mixture over medium-low heat, stirring constantly, until it thickens and begins to pull away from the sides of the skillet. This may take about 10-15 minutes.
6. Once the date mixture reaches a thick, dough-like consistency, remove it from the heat and let it cool slightly.
7. While the mixture is still warm, divide it into equal-sized balls and flatten them slightly to form discs or patties.
8. Place a toasted nut in the center of each date disc and press it down gently.
9. Allow the Kleeja Halwa to cool completely before serving. You can store them in an airtight container at room temperature for several days.

Enjoy the rich and flavorful Kleeja Halwa as a delicious sweet treat during festive occasions or as a delightful snack any time of the year! Adjust the sweetness and spice levels according to your taste preferences.

Roz bil Khalta

Ingredients:

- 2 cups Basmati rice, rinsed and soaked for 30 minutes
- 4 cups water
- 2 tablespoons ghee or vegetable oil
- 1 onion, finely chopped
- 2 cloves garlic, minced
- 1 pound lamb or beef, cut into small cubes
- 1 teaspoon ground turmeric
- 1 teaspoon ground cumin
- 1 teaspoon ground coriander
- 1/2 teaspoon ground cinnamon
- Salt and black pepper, to taste
- 1/2 cup chopped fresh cilantro (coriander leaves)
- 1/2 cup chopped fresh parsley
- Toasted almonds or pine nuts, for garnish (optional)

Instructions:

1. In a large pot or Dutch oven, heat the ghee or vegetable oil over medium heat. Add the chopped onion and minced garlic, and sauté until softened and fragrant.
2. Add the cubed lamb or beef to the pot and cook until browned on all sides.
3. Stir in the ground turmeric, ground cumin, ground coriander, ground cinnamon, salt, and black pepper. Cook for another minute until the spices are fragrant.
4. Drain the soaked Basmati rice and add it to the pot, stirring to coat the rice with the spice mixture.
5. Pour the water into the pot, ensuring that the rice is fully submerged in the liquid.
6. Bring the mixture to a boil, then reduce the heat to low. Cover the pot and let the rice simmer gently for about 15-20 minutes, or until the rice is cooked through and fluffy.
7. Once the rice is cooked, remove the pot from the heat and let it sit, covered, for a few minutes to allow the flavors to meld.
8. Fluff the rice with a fork and transfer it to a serving platter.
9. Garnish the Roz bil Khalta with chopped fresh cilantro, chopped fresh parsley, and toasted almonds or pine nuts, if desired.
10. Serve the Khalta Rice hot as a main dish or as a side dish with your favorite meat or vegetable dishes.

Enjoy the flavorful and aromatic Roz bil Khalta as a delicious and satisfying meal for your family and friends! Adjust the spices and seasoning according to your taste preferences.

Harees Dajaj

Ingredients:

- 1 cup whole wheat grains
- 1 pound chicken pieces (with bone-in for added flavor)
- 6 cups water
- 1 teaspoon ground cumin
- 1 teaspoon ground coriander
- 1/2 teaspoon ground cinnamon
- Salt, to taste
- Ghee or butter, for serving (optional)
- Ground black pepper, for serving (optional)

Instructions:

1. Rinse the whole wheat grains under cold water until the water runs clear. Drain well.
2. In a large pot, combine the rinsed wheat grains, chicken pieces, and water. Bring to a boil over high heat.
3. Once boiling, reduce the heat to low and let the mixture simmer, partially covered, for about 1 hour, stirring occasionally to prevent sticking.
4. After an hour, the wheat grains should start breaking down and becoming mushy. Continue cooking and stirring until the mixture resembles a thick porridge-like consistency. This may take another 1-2 hours.
5. Once the mixture has thickened, add the ground cumin, ground coriander, ground cinnamon, and salt to taste. Stir well to combine.
6. Continue cooking the Harees Dajaj over low heat for another 30-60 minutes, or until the wheat and chicken are fully cooked and well incorporated.
7. Adjust the seasoning if needed and remove the pot from the heat.
8. Serve the Harees Dajaj hot, drizzled with ghee or butter and a sprinkle of ground black pepper, if desired.

Enjoy the warm and comforting Chicken Harees as a nutritious and satisfying meal, especially during cooler months or as a dish to share with loved ones during gatherings and celebrations. Adjust the spices and consistency according to your preferences.

Murabyan

Ingredients:

- 2 pounds ripe mangoes or citrus fruits (such as oranges or lemons)
- 4 cups granulated sugar
- 1 cup water
- 2 cinnamon sticks
- 4-5 whole cloves
- 1 teaspoon ground cardamom
- 1 teaspoon ground ginger
- 1/2 teaspoon ground nutmeg
- Juice of 1 lemon (for citrus fruits only)

Instructions:

1. Wash and peel the mangoes or citrus fruits. If using mangoes, cut them into small cubes. If using citrus fruits, slice them thinly.
2. In a large pot, combine the fruit with sugar, water, cinnamon sticks, cloves, ground cardamom, ground ginger, and ground nutmeg.
3. If using citrus fruits, add the lemon juice to the pot as well.
4. Place the pot over medium heat and bring the mixture to a boil, stirring occasionally to dissolve the sugar.
5. Once the mixture comes to a boil, reduce the heat to low and let it simmer gently for about 1-2 hours, or until the fruits are soft and the syrup has thickened to your desired consistency. Stir occasionally to prevent sticking.
6. As the mixture cooks, skim off any foam that rises to the surface.
7. Once the Murabyan has reached the desired consistency, remove the pot from the heat and let it cool slightly.
8. Transfer the Murabyan to clean, sterilized jars and seal tightly.
9. Let the Murabyan cool completely before storing it in the refrigerator. It will continue to thicken as it cools.
10. Serve the Murabyan as a sweet and tangy condiment or dessert, or use it as a filling for pastries or desserts.

Enjoy the delightful flavors of homemade Murabyan as a delicious addition to your meals or as a thoughtful homemade gift for friends and family. Adjust the sweetness and spices according to your taste preferences.

Jareesh Halib

Ingredients:

- 1 cup cracked wheat (jareesh)
- 4 cups milk
- 2 cups water
- 1/4 cup sugar (adjust to taste)
- 1/2 teaspoon ground cardamom
- 1/4 teaspoon ground cinnamon
- Pinch of salt
- Chopped nuts (such as almonds, pistachios, or walnuts), for garnish (optional)
- Raisins or dried fruits, for garnish (optional)

Instructions:

1. Rinse the cracked wheat under cold water until the water runs clear. Drain well.
2. In a large pot, combine the rinsed cracked wheat, milk, and water. Bring to a boil over medium-high heat.
3. Once boiling, reduce the heat to low and let the mixture simmer, stirring occasionally to prevent sticking, for about 30-40 minutes, or until the cracked wheat is cooked through and the mixture has thickened to a porridge-like consistency.
4. Stir in the sugar, ground cardamom, ground cinnamon, and a pinch of salt. Adjust the sweetness and spices to taste.
5. Continue cooking the Jareesh Halib over low heat for another 10-15 minutes, stirring occasionally, until the flavors are well combined and the porridge has reached your desired consistency.
6. Once cooked, remove the pot from the heat and let the Jareesh Halib cool slightly.
7. Serve the Jareesh Halib warm, garnished with chopped nuts and raisins or dried fruits, if desired.

Enjoy the creamy and aromatic Jareesh Halib as a comforting breakfast or dessert option. You can also experiment with additional flavorings such as rose water or orange blossom water for a fragrant twist. Adjust the sweetness and thickness of the porridge according to your preferences.

www.ingramcontent.com/pod-product-compliance
Lightning Source LLC
LaVergne TN
LVHW062047070526
838201LV00080B/2109